SWEET
CHERRY PIE
PUMPKIN PIE
Strawberry Pie
PECAN PIE
"in PIE we crust."
tara, the pie queen

KEEP YOUR FORK,
THERE'S PIE!

TARA ROYER STEELE

PHOTOGRAPHY BY LORI SPARKMAN

TEN PEAKS PRESS®
EUGENE, OR

The author is represented by Alive Literary Agency, www.aliveliterary.com

Photography by Lori Sparkman
Cover design by Faceout Studio, Molly von Borstel
Interior design by Faceout Studio, Paul Nielsen
Fork graphic © Vasya Kobelev / Shutterstock; Pie graphic © A-spring / Shutterstock

For bulk or special sales, please call 1 (800) 547-8979. Email: CustomerService@hhpbooks.com

TEN PEAKS PRESS is a federally registered trademark of The Hawkins Children's LLC. Harvest House Publishers, Inc., is the exclusive licensee of this trademark.

Keep Your Fork, There's Pie!

Published by Ten Peaks Press, an imprint of Harvest House Publishers
Eugene, Oregon 97408

ISBN 978-0-7369-8982-4 (hardcover)
ISBN 978-0-7369-8983-1 (eBook)

Library of Congress Control Number: 2025931162

Printed in China

25 26 27 28 29 30 31 32 33 / DC / 10 9 8 7 6 5 4 3 2

To my mom and dad,
who took a leap of faith and loaded
up their whole family to take over
a tiny café with two pie recipes.

To my mom,
Dr. Karen Royer, who taught
me to invite everyone to the table,
love like Jesus, celebrate *big*,
and do all things *boldly*!

And to my dad,
who taught me to persevere through
the hard and refine a true flavor palate.

I have to give the *biggest*
shout out to my boys:
Rick, Brayden, and Bentley.
I love getting to sit around the
table with y'all. My favorite
conversations happen there.

CONTENTS

INTRODUCTION

Hey y'all! I'm Tara Royer Steele, a.k.a. "The Pie Queen," and I have been in the pie business for 38 years. I'm so excited to share with you not only these recipes but the stories and love that have been poured into this book. At a young age, I started baking loaves of bread and cookies to sell at church on Sunday. In 1987, my parents took a leap of faith and moved our family to Round Top, Texas, where they took over a little café on the town square. I was 12 years old when I started working alongside my three younger brothers at the café. I waited on tables and helped wherever needed. Growing up in our family business, I learned to persevere in the hard and watched God reveal Himself to me through pie and gathering around the table. My mom taught me to see everyone who walked through the doors as an image bearer of Christ and modeled the value that everyone is invited. My dad taught me you can take what God has provided and put your creative spin on it. He taught me about depth of flavor and adding an extra dash of seasoning. My brothers taught me to love deeply, and I consider them treasures from God. I got to own that little café for about 18 years and passed the torch on to my brother JB and his wife, Jamie-Len, in 2018.

I am married to my knight in shining armor, Rick Steele, and we have two boys, Brayden and Bentley. Rick and I have always shared a dream to work alongside each other. With our combined ingredients, and Christ as our foundation, we make the best pie. We opened Royers Pie Haven, also located in Round Top, in 2011. There, I felt like I could be my true, authentic self. I gained the confidence to create most of the recipes I'm sharing with you in this cookbook. The Pie Haven is small and has no kitchen, so we bake our pies, pastries, mail-order pies, family dinner casseroles, and catered meals at our Bake Shop at All Things Acres in Brenham, Texas. All Things Acres is also home to our nonprofit, Gather n Grace, which aims to help everyone get to God's best for their lives—mentally, physically, and spiritually.

This cookbook will show you the grace that comes with baking, just like the grace Christ has for you. It doesn't have to be complicated to be full of joy. My prayer is that every time someone makes one of these pies, they will be gently reminded of the sweet truth that they are loved. Don't forget to keep your fork, there's pie!

ROYERS
PIE HAVEN
COFFEE
COLD DRINKS
LUNCH
PIES
BAKED GOODS
COFFEE
Savory Pies:
VEGGIE
HEE HAW
CHICKEN MARGHERITA
CHICKEN POT PIE

PIE CRUST AND TOPPINGS

{A Smidgen of Faith}

Jesus says in Matthew 17:20, "Truly, I say to you, if you have faith like a grain of mustard seed, you will say to this mountain, 'Move from here to there,' and it will move, and nothing will be impossible for you" (ESV). There have been times in my life when my faith wasn't even the size of a mustard seed; it was more like a speck of sugar. And my attitude didn't taste like sugar either; it probably tasted more like salt. There have been times in my faith that I've fallen to my knees, crying out for mercy because the mountain was so big. The mountain wouldn't move because I kept trying to do it alone. There have also been times in my journey when my faith was so big I could be at the top of the mountain and jump! The best thing about Jesus is that His well never runs dry, and we only need a drop of water to renew us. He is the only foundation we need. The recipes in this section are the foundation on which Jesus built our business, from simple ingredients like flour, sugar, water, salt, shortening, butter, and oats. These recipes are like a mustard seed, the starting point for faith, so as a starting point for your baking, always have these ingredients on hand to create a beautiful foundation.

ROYERS PIE CRUST

PREP TIME: 15 minutes **YIELD:** 3 (1 lb.) dough balls

INGREDIENTS

¼ tsp. salt
1 cup water
5 cups all-purpose flour, plus more for kneading
1 cup Crisco shortening
1 cup butter, cubed, at room temperature

DIRECTIONS

Dissolve the salt in the water and set aside. Measure the flour into a large bowl. Cut the shortening and butter into the flour with a fork or pastry cutter. When the mixture is crumbly, add all the salt water and knead until the water is absorbed. Add several tablespoons of flour and knead the dough until it pulls away from your hands cleanly. Roll the dough into three balls and place each in a plastic bag. Freeze until ready to use. When you are ready to use the dough, set it out to thaw for 3 to 4 hours or place it in your refrigerator overnight. The dough rolls out easiest at room temperature.

I remember we didn't know anything about pie when we moved to Round Top. Our sweet friend Sharon Hopkins shared her grandmother's pie crust recipe with us and it's been a staple ever since. I'm grateful that when we walk in our calling, God brings who we need to keep walking in the path He's provided.

For many years, we always used Crisco as the fat in our pie crust, but recently, we have added butter to the recipe for a tad more flavor and to give the crust a more golden touch.

CHOCOLATE PIE CRUST

PREP TIME: 20 minutes **YIELD:** 1 (9-inch) pie crust

INGREDIENTS

2⅔ cups flour
⅓ cup cocoa powder
3½ T. sugar
1 tsp. salt
1 cup cold unsalted butter, cubed
¼ to ½ cup cold water

DIRECTIONS

Add the flour, cocoa powder, sugar, and salt to a large bowl or food processor and mix well. Cut in the butter until the mixture is like sand in texture. Add the cold water, starting with ¼ cup and adding 1 tablespoon at a time until the dough is not dry and not sticky. Form into a disc shape and wrap in plastic wrap. Refrigerate for 30 minutes or until needed.

We don't use this crust in many of our pies, but it would be fantastic with Cherry, Strawberry Rhubarb, Sweet 'n' Salty, or Texas Trash. Wouldn't it be fabulous to roll out into cinnamon sticks? Roll the dough to a ¼-inch thickness, add butter with cinnamon and sugar, and bake at 325°F for 20 to 25 minutes.

HERB PIE CRUST

PREP TIME: 15 minutes **YIELD:** 3 (1 lb.) dough balls

INGREDIENTS

¼ tsp. salt
1 cup water
5 cups all-purpose flour, plus more for kneading
4 tsp. Louise's Herb Mix
2 cups Crisco shortening

DIRECTIONS

Dissolve the salt in the water and set aside. In a large bowl, combine the flour and herb mix. Cut the shortening into the flour mixture with a fork or pastry cutter. When the mixture is crumbly, add all the salt water and knead until the water is absorbed. Add several tablespoons of flour and knead the dough until it pulls away from your hands cleanly. Roll the dough into three balls and place each in a ziplock bag. Freeze until ready to use. When you are ready to use the dough, set it out to thaw for 3 to 4 hours or place it in your refrigerator overnight. The dough rolls out easiest at room temperature.

LOUISE'S HERB MIX

PREP TIME: 10 minutes **YIELD:** 3 cups

INGREDIENTS

1 cup garlic powder
⅔ cup dried dill weed
⅓ cup marjoram
⅓ cup dried basil leaves
⅓ cup dried thyme leaves
⅛ cup black pepper
Pinch of cayenne

DIRECTIONS

Mix all ingredients in a bowl and store in an airtight container for a long time! You may want to wear a face mask; this herb mix will make you sneeze!

I don't remember how Louise and I met in the first place, although it was never in person, only by phone or email. I would order Louise's Herb Mix for our herb butter at the café. Over time, we built a beautiful relationship. One day I got a call from her son that Louise had passed and she wanted me to have her recipe. I love that a simple conversation to order herbs became a friendship that was planted, cultivated, and watered over the years.

CHOCOLATE CORNFLAKE CRUST

PREP TIME: 10 minutes **YIELD:** 1 (9-inch) pie crust

INGREDIENTS

7 T. butter
¼ cup brown sugar
2 oz. unsweetened baking chocolate
½ cup semi-sweet chocolate chips
3 cups cornflakes
⅓ cup chopped pecans

DIRECTIONS

In a medium saucepan, melt the butter, brown sugar, and both chocolates over low heat. Stir constantly until thoroughly combined and the sugar is dissolved. Turn off heat. In a large bowl, combine the cornflakes and pecans; pour the warm chocolate mixture over the flakes, gently stirring until the flakes are thoroughly coated. Spray a 9-inch pie pan with cooking spray and gently press the coated flakes into the pie pan. Place in the freezer until firm, about 1 hour.

I love using this crust for ice cream. Chocolate ice cream with strawberries, coffee ice cream with chocolate sauce . . . the combinations are endless. I bet it would be wonderful with your favorite cream pie.

OREO CRUST

PREP TIME: 5 minutes **YIELD:** 1 (9-inch) pie crust

INGREDIENTS

18 Oreos
¼ cup butter, melted

DIRECTIONS

Add Oreos and butter to a food processor. Pulse until the Oreos are broken into coarse pieces—I like big, chunky pieces. Press into your 9-inch pie pan.

Do I need to say anything about Oreos as a foundation for your pie? Shhhh, don't tell the cookies in this book, but I love Oreos! And, no, I don't take them apart, I love 'em just as they are!

TEXAS TRASH CRUST

Good luck with making this crust and not sneaking a bite before it makes it to the pie pan. My mom made Rice Krispies Treats often. She would call us all into the kitchen and we would eat them hot before they even made it into the pan. Those are sweet memories I'll keep holding onto.

PREP TIME: 10 minutes **YIELD:** 1 (9-inch) pie crust

INGREDIENTS

- ½ cup butter
- 5 oz. marshmallows
- 2½ cups Rice Krispies
- ¼ cup unsweetened coconut flakes
- ¼ cup crushed graham crackers
- ¼ cup crushed pretzels
- ¼ cup chocolate chips
- ¼ cup Kraft caramel bits

DIRECTIONS

Melt the butter in a large saucepan over medium heat. When the butter is nearly melted, add the marshmallows. Stir until marshmallows are nearly melted, and mix in the Rice Krispies. Add the coconut, graham crackers, pretzels, chocolate, and caramel bits. Stir until combined. Press mixture into a greased 9-inch pie pan.

BUTTERCREAM FROSTING

PREP TIME: 10 minutes **YIELD:** 5 cups

Before we moved to Round Top, I loved to make cakes and took a Wilton cake decorating class when I was nine. This is a spin-off of the icing we would make in class. We use this for cupcake war birthday parties at the Bake Shop, our Sin-namon Rolls, and Pie-wiches (page 135).

INGREDIENTS

- 1 cup butter, softened
- 4½ cups powdered sugar
- 2 tsp. vanilla
- 2 T. milk

DIRECTIONS

Combine all ingredients in a stand mixer and blend until smooth and creamy. Store in an airtight container for up to 30 days.

TARA'S CINNAMON WHIPPED CREAM

PREP TIME: 10 minutes **YIELD:** 2 cups

INGREDIENTS

1 pint heavy whipping cream
1 cup powdered sugar
1 tsp. vanilla
1 tsp. cinnamon

DIRECTIONS

Pour the heavy whipping cream into a stand mixer with a whisk attachment. Whisk until the cream begins to froth. Add the powdered sugar and whisk until soft peaks form. Add the vanilla and cinnamon, and whisk until combined. Refrigerate in an airtight container until you eat it or for up to 7 days.

This whipped cream is a staple around our home, Bake Shop, and catering. It pairs well with a big ole bowl of fresh fruit, sweet pies, and is PIE-rrific with Berry Scones (page 121).

CLARISSA'S COLD BREW

PREP TIME: 24 hours **YIELD:** 3 cups

INGREDIENTS

1 cup medium roast ground coffee
24 oz. water

DIRECTIONS

Put the grounds in a coffee filter and tie them with a rubber band. Fill a pitcher with water and soak the grounds for 24 hours. Remove the coffee and squeeze the grounds to get all that goodness. Be careful not to break the filter!

Clarissa has worked with us for many years; she knows the ins and outs of all the things. She took a leap of faith and left her secure pharmaceutical job to run Royers Pie Haven. We had no idea how we would pay her at the time, but the Lord made a way. Rick and I owned a coffee roasting company and would bottle our cold brew and ship it all over the U.S. Clarissa and Rick worked many hours to PIE-fect it for shipping. Maybe we should bring it back!

CRUMBLE CAKE TOPPING

PREP TIME: 5 minutes **YIELD:** Tops 1 (9-inch) pie

INGREDIENTS

1¼ cups yellow cake mix
9 T. brown sugar
1⅓ tsp. cinnamon
3 T. butter, melted

DIRECTIONS

Combine all ingredients in a large mixing bowl. Add to the top of a pie and spread it to cover the filling, then bake as directed for the pie.

OAT TOPPING

PREP TIME: 5 minutes **YIELD:** Tops 1 (9-inch) pie

INGREDIENTS

1 cup brown sugar
¾ tsp. cinnamon
½ cup butter, softened
1 cup old-fashioned oats
½ cup flour
⅛ tsp. salt
Pinch of nutmeg

DIRECTIONS

Combine all ingredients in a large mixing bowl. Add to the top of a pie and spread it to cover the filling, then bake as directed for the pie.

STREUSEL TOPPING

PREP TIME: 5 minutes **YIELD:** Tops 1 (9-inch) pie

INGREDIENTS

1 cup brown sugar
½ cup pecan pieces
3 T. flour
2 tsp. cinnamon
2 tsp. butter, melted

DIRECTIONS

Combine all ingredients in a large mixing bowl. Add to the top of a pie and spread it to cover the filling, then bake as directed for the pie.

PANTRY STAPLES

These are items I never run out of. (It does help that I have 500 pounds of flour readily available to me!)

- Flour: I always buy the cheapest all-purpose flour.
- Eggs
- Butter: Unsalted is my go-to; I prefer to add salt if necessary.
- Crisco: To make a great crust, this is my go-to.
- Light brown sugar: I always keep this around but I rarely have dark brown sugar in my kitchen.
- Granulated sugar: Can't have enough!
- Powdered sugar
- Cocoa powder: Always a must; my favorite brand is Ghirardelli.
- Unsweetened coconut flakes
- Salt: table salt and coarse sea salt
- Milk chocolate chips
- Kraft caramel bits
- Pecan pieces
- Pecan halves
- Dairy: heavy whipping cream, half-and-half, sour cream, mozzarella, feta, and shredded cheddar
- Vanilla: I love vanilla; it goes in everything. I always keep a few bottles around.
- Almond extract
- Cinnamon
- Nutmeg

BAKING SUPPLIES

- Measuring cups and spoons: Can't have enough. Okay, I buy cute ones, but they have metal, glass, and plastic.
- Mixing bowls: Metal bowls are great for whipping cream or eggs. A glass bowl is my favorite.
- Rubber spatula/scraper
- Metal whisk
- Tongs
- Disposable rubber gloves for handling raw meats
- Nonstick sauté pans
- Silicone rubber pastry brush
- Kitchen scissors: I love having these for cubing raw chicken.
- Rolling pin: I love a marble pin.
- Peeler
- Cutting board
- Knives: Cutco is the knife brand we use at home. We have every knife you can think of, but we always have a chef's knife and one for paring.
- Foil, metal, and glass pie pans: These are always stored in the drawers. Metal gets hotter faster but takes longer to cook. Glass ones retain heat longer and are great when you want to keep your pie warmer at the table.
- Cookie sheets
- Digital scale: I keep a few around my kitchen so my measurements will be precise.

ROYER FAMILY SIGNATURE PIES

{A Pinch of Perfection}

I am a recovering perfectionist. When I met my husband, Rick, I would make my kitchen spotless every day. Everything had to be in its perfect place. I'm sure he began questioning what he had gotten himself into. After 18 years of marriage, having boys, and building an emPIEr together, I don't have time for perfection. I've had to learn to rise above it, because the Lord has something better for me. Of course, I struggle still, but I see that seeking constant perfection keeps me in a loop of failure. The Lord doesn't want me to strive for perfection; He wants me to thrive in relationships with Him and others.

What does this have to do with pie? I didn't go to college or culinary school; I learned everything about business and baking through trial and error, which was a path I didn't pick. *But God.* I was struggling one day with where the Lord had me after He had just released Rick and me from the café. I believed I had nothing to offer the world. A friend reminded me to take what I had learned—skills, talent, and experiences—and put my creative spin on it. I remembered the recipes, events, and signature pies that I had been a part of, and while they weren't perfect, they were *just right*. They had carried me to right here, exactly where the Lord wanted me. When we surrender all our control, fears, and perfection to Him and walk in our calling, He will bring the people to cheer us on and buy the pie. Even if it's not perfect in my eyes, it's perfect in His.

Here is a compilation of all the pies the Lord insPIEred and that became a signature in our businesses; they are a pinch of perfection.

BUTTERSCOTCH CHIP PIE

PREP TIME: 15 minutes **BAKE TIME:** 60 minutes

YIELD: 1 (9-inch) pie

INGREDIENTS

1 (1 lb.) Royers dough ball (page 11) or 9-inch unbaked pie shell
1 cup sugar
1 cup light brown sugar
1 cup flour
2 eggs, slightly beaten
½ cup butter, melted
½ cup chopped pecans
½ cup butterscotch chips

DIRECTIONS

Preheat the oven to 325°F. Roll out the dough ball until it is ¼ inch thick and then lay it in a 9-inch pie pan. Press dough into the base of the pie pan and crimp the edge with your two forefingers. In a mixing bowl, combine the sugar, brown sugar, and flour. Stir in the eggs and butter, mixing well. Fold in the pecans and butterscotch chips. Spread the filling in your pie crust and bake for 60 minutes or until the knife comes out clean.

This is a sleeper on the menu, but we might have some angry customers if we remove it. Former Texas Governor Rick Perry has a home in Round Top, and this is his favorite pie. If you like butterscotch, you'll love this pie! It is best warmed and served with vanilla ice cream.

PEANUT BUTTER WHITE TRASH PIE

PREP TIME: 15 minutes **BAKE TIME:** 45 minutes

YIELD: 1 (9-inch) pie

INGREDIENTS

1 (1 lb.) Royers dough ball (page 11) or 9-inch unbaked pie shell
1 cup crushed graham crackers
1 cup crushed salted pretzels
1 cup white chocolate chips
1 cup unsweetened coconut flakes
1 cup Kraft caramel bits
1 cup creamy peanut butter, softened
½ cup butter, melted
1 (14 oz.) can sweetened condensed milk

DIRECTIONS

Preheat the oven to 325°F. Roll out the dough ball until it is ¼ inch thick and lay it in a 9-inch pie pan. Press dough into the base of the pie pan and crimp the edge with your two forefingers. Toss all dry ingredients in a medium mixing bowl and mix until combined. Add in wet ingredients and stir until all mixed in. Pour ingredients into pie crust and press into pie shell. Bake for 45 minutes. Let the pie cool before cutting.

I don't love cleaning measuring cups that have shortening in them. To save cleaning time, I line the cup with a paper towel and then scoop the shortening into the cup. It pops right out of your measuring cup, and the cup is clean!

I was a vendor at the Texas Pie Fest, and one of the customers tried the Texas Trash Pie (page 28) and said, "You should try different ingredients and come up with other trashy recipes!" Good idea! Thanks to him, you now have one of my favorites, especially warmed and served with vanilla ice cream. If you like peanut butter, it's better than the original! Oh, wouldn't chocolate ice cream be good!

BENTLEY'S RED VELVET OREO PIE

PREP TIME: 15 minutes **BAKE TIME:** 45 minutes

YIELD: 1 (9-inch) pie

INGREDIENTS

1 (1 lb.) Royers dough ball (page 11) or 9-inch unbaked pie shell
½ cup butter
¾ cup sugar
2 eggs
2 tsp. vanilla
2 tsp. cocoa powder
1 cup flour
½ tsp. salt
⅜ tsp. baking soda
1 cup milk chocolate chips
1½ cups crumbled Oreos

DIRECTIONS

Preheat the oven to 325°F. Roll out the dough ball until it is ¼ inch thick and lay it in a 9-inch pie pan. Press dough into the base of the pie pan and crimp the edge with your two forefingers. In a stand mixer, cream the butter and sugar. Add the eggs and vanilla. Mix thoroughly with the cocoa powder, flour, salt, and baking soda. Fold in the chocolate chips and Oreos. Pour filling into the shell and bake for 45 minutes.

At the Royers Pie Haven, we call the girls who work behind the counter "pie chicks." Brynn, a pie chick, loves Oreos and anything red velvet. She challenged me to create a pie with these flavors. I got to work in the kitchen and didn't write the recipe down before she got to try it—a hazard of living with a house full of boys! I re-created the pie, and the recipe is perfected now and a fan favorite. My son Bentley doesn't love pie and is not shy to tell you he doesn't like it, but this one has changed his perspective.

PIE IS LOVE

TEXAS TRASH PIE

PREP TIME: 15 minutes **BAKE TIME:** 45 minutes

YIELD: 1 (9-inch) pie

INGREDIENTS

- 1 (1 lb.) Royers dough ball (page 11) or 9-inch unbaked pie shell
- 1 cup crumbled graham crackers
- 1 cup crumbled salted pretzels
- 1 cup chocolate chips
- 1 cup unsweetened coconut flakes
- 1 cup Kraft caramel bits
- ½ cup butter, melted
- 1 (14 oz.) can sweetened condensed milk

DIRECTIONS

Preheat the oven to 325°F. Roll out the dough ball until it is ¼ inch thick and lay it in a 9-inch pie pan. Press dough into the base of the pie pan and crimp the edge with your two forefingers. Toss all dry ingredients in a medium mixing bowl and mix until combined. Add in wet ingredients and stir until all mixed in. Pour ingredients into pie crust and press into pie shell. Bake for 45 minutes. Let the pie cool before cutting.

Oh, Texas Trash, you are everyone's favorite. If you don't like one of the ingredients, take it out and add a bit more of another. Even if you don't like coconut, you'll love it! Trust me on this one. I think it's fantastic with a scoop of coffee ice cream.

TARA'S CHOCOLATE CHIP PIE

PREP TIME: 15 minutes **BAKE TIME:** 35 to 45 minutes

YIELD: 1 (9-inch) pie

INGREDIENTS

1 (1 lb.) Royers dough ball (page 11) or 9-inch unbaked pie shell
⅓ cup butter, melted
⅓ cup shortening
⅔ cup brown sugar
⅔ cup sugar
1 egg
1 tsp. vinegar
⅛ tsp. almond extract
1½ tsp. vanilla
⅓ tsp. salt
½ tsp. baking soda
1⅓ cup flour
1 cup chocolate chips
⅔ cup pecan pieces

DIRECTIONS

Preheat the oven to 325°F. Roll out the dough ball until it is ¼ inch thick and lay it in a 9-inch pie pan. Press the pie dough into the base of the pie pan and crimp the edges with your two forefingers. In a stand mixer, cream butter, shortening, brown sugar, and sugar. Add the egg, vinegar, almond extract, and vanilla. In a separate bowl, combine the salt, baking soda, and flour. Scoop the dry ingredients into the wet mixture and mix until blended. Fold in the chocolate chips and pecans. Pour ingredients into pie crust and press into pie shell. Bake for 35 to 45 minutes.

Bud's Chocolate Chip Pie was the first pie my dad made on his own and put on the menu at the café all those years ago. It was a favorite with fans for years. When God released me from my duty at the café, I believed I had nothing to offer the world and wondered, "Who the heck would hire me?" I was sharing with a friend, and she told me, "Take what you have learned, walk in your giftings, and put your own creative spin on it!" That's what I did when creating Tara's Chocolate Chip Pie.

SWEET 'N' SALTY PIE

PREP TIME: 15 minutes **BAKE TIME:** 35 to 45 minutes

YIELD: 2 (9-inch) pies

INGREDIENTS

2 (1 lb.) Royers dough balls (page 11) or 2 (9-inch) unbaked pie shells
½ cup butter
1½ cups sugar
2 eggs
2 tsp. vanilla
1 cup flour
⅓ cup cocoa powder
⅓ tsp. baking soda
¼ tsp. salt
¾ cup Kraft caramel bits
½ cup chocolate chips
¼ tsp. coarse sea salt

DIRECTIONS

Preheat the oven to 325°F. Roll out the dough balls until each one is ¼ inch thick and lay them in two 9-inch pie pans. Press dough into the base of each pie pan and crimp the edge with your two forefingers. In a large bowl, cream the butter, sugar, eggs, and vanilla until the mixture is light and fluffy. Combine the flour, cocoa powder, baking soda, and salt in a separate bowl. Stir the flour mixture into the butter mixture until well blended. Mix in the caramel bits and chocolate chips. Press the filling into the pie shells and sprinkle with the sea salt. Bake for 35 to 45 minutes. If your knife doesn't come out clean, it's okay! It will be hard to resist, but let the pies cool before slicing.

Oh, Sweet 'n' Salty, you will always be my favorite. This pie started as a cookie at Royers Pie Haven, and since we made other cookie pies, we decided to try a Sweet 'n' Salty pie! This is one of our most popular pies. Who wouldn't love a dense, fudgy brownie with caramel and sea salt?

SNICKERDOODLE PIE

PREP TIME: 30 minutes **BAKE TIME:** 35 minutes

YIELD: 1 (9-inch) pie

INGREDIENTS

1 (1 lb.) Royers dough ball (page 11) or 9-inch unbaked pie shell

Snickerdoodle Dough

½ cup sugar
¼ cup brown sugar
½ cup butter, softened
½ tsp. vanilla
1½ cups flour
¼ cup milk
1 egg
½ tsp. cinnamon
¼ tsp. baking soda
¼ tsp. cream of tartar

Dusting Sugar

1 T. cinnamon
⅓ cup sugar

Cream Cheese Filling

4 oz. cream cheese, softened
½ cup sugar
1 egg
1 tsp. vanilla

DIRECTIONS

Preheat the oven to 325°F. Roll out the dough ball until it is ¼ inch thick and lay it in a 9-inch pie pan. Press the pie dough into the base of the pie pan and crimp the edges with your two forefingers.

In a stand mixer, cream the sugar, brown sugar, butter, and vanilla. Add the flour, milk, egg, cinnamon, baking soda, and cream of tartar and blend until it forms a soft dough.

Press half of the snickerdoodle dough into the pie crust to cover the bottom. Stir together the cinnamon and sugar for dusting and sprinkle over the snickerdoodle layer of the pie.

Combine the cream cheese, sugar, egg, and vanilla in a separate bowl until creamy. Spoon the cream cheese mixture on top of the snickerdoodle and sugar layers and spread to cover the pie.

Press the remaining snickerdoodle dough on top of the cream cheese mixture. Bake for 35 minutes or until the top of the pie is golden brown. Remove from the oven and cool before serving.

Kids will love this pie. It has just the right amount of sugar and spice, and everything is nice. I love the softness of the snickerdoodle filling combined with the sweetness of the cream cheese. This would be a great pie to test out your creativity by adding cinnamon chips or even caramel bits.

SWEET PIES

{A Drop of Love}

There's something sweet about creating a pie from scratch. It is a labor of love that results in a sweet treat that is hard to resist, especially warmed and served with your favorite ice cream. From rolling out the imperfect (yes, nothing is perfect) pie crust to filling it with a luscious fruit or creamy chess filling, every step is infused with love and kindness.

When I ask others what scares them about making a pie, they say, "The crust." In 1 Thessalonians 5:16-18, we are instructed to "rejoice always, pray constantly, give thanks in everything; for this is God's will for you in Christ Jesus." In my life, I have prayed without ceasing about pie. Many moments weren't sweet, but through it all I've seen His sweetness in my life.

Imagine yourself standing at your kitchen counter and wondering how these few items—flour, shortening, water, and salt—can create something so sweet. But Jesus is standing next to you, talking you through making a pie crust and gently reminding you that He is with you through it all. What if you surrendered all to Him—even making a pie?

One of my favorite sayings is, "Trust the process." You might think your pie doesn't look great, but it is a beautiful masterpiece when it comes out of the fire. So make that pie, even if you feel intimidated, because He's with you through it all and will create the sweetest memories of sharing the pie around the table.

TEXAS TRASH CHOCOLATE CREAM PIE

PREP TIME: 30 minutes **YIELD:** 1 (9-inch) pie

INGREDIENTS

1 Texas Trash Crust (page 14)

Chocolate Filling

1½ cups powdered sugar

½ cup cocoa powder

1 tsp. vanilla

8 oz. cream cheese, softened

½ cup butter

4 oz. semi-sweet chocolate chips

3 cups Tara's Cinnamon Whipped Cream (page 15)

Topping

2 cups Tara's Cinnamon Whipped Cream

Cocoa powder for dusting

DIRECTIONS

Have your Texas Trash Crust at the ready, then prepare the chocolate filling. In a stand mixer, mix the powdered sugar, cocoa powder, vanilla, and cream cheese. In a microwaveable bowl, melt the butter and chocolate chips in 30-second intervals, stirring each time until the chocolate is completely melted. Pour the chocolate mixture into the cream cheese mixture and combine. Fold in the 3 cups whipped cream. Pour into the pie shell. Top with the additional 2 cups whipped cream and sprinkle with cocoa powder. Refrigerate for 4 hours or overnight.

Y'all, this pie is like the cream to your coffee or ice cream to your pie. The chocolate cream in that Texas Trash Pie Crust is a heavenly match! It's rich and decadent, you don't need much, and it's worth the calories.

COLD BREW COFFEE PIE

PREP TIME: 24 hours + 4 hours **YIELD:** 2 (9-inch) pies

INGREDIENTS

2 Oreo Crusts (page 13)

Filling

1 (5 oz.) pkg. vanilla pudding mix
¼ cup sweetened condensed milk
1 T. vanilla
1 cup Clarissa's Cold Brew (page 15) or store-bought cold brew
2 cups Tara's Cinnamon Whipped Cream (page 15) or 1 (12-oz.) tub Cool Whip
½ cup heavy whipping cream

DIRECTIONS

Note: Remember to prep Clarissa's Cold Brew 24 hours in advance.

Have both Oreo Crusts at the ready. For the filling, combine all ingredients and pour evenly into the pie pans. Chill for 4 hours before serving.

I love walking into Royers Pie Haven and smelling fresh brewed coffee and hearing the sound of the espresso machine whipping up the PIE-fect latte. This pie doesn't have an overly strong coffee flavor; it is just right! It is best served chilled, but throw it in the freezer for a PIE-rrific treat during those hot summer days. Or, maybe have it for breakfast with your coffee. As my dad, The Pieman himself, says, "LITS." **L**ife **i**s **t**oo **s**hort to not eat pie!

OATMEAL CREAM PIES

PREP TIME: 20 minutes **BAKE TIME:** 10 to 12 minutes

YIELD: 12 cream pies

INGREDIENTS

Oatmeal Cookies

1¼ cups butter
1 cup packed dark brown sugar
½ cup granulated sugar
1 egg
2 tsp. vanilla
½ T. dark molasses
2½ cups flour
3 cups quick oats
½ tsp. kosher salt
½ tsp. cinnamon
1 tsp. baking soda

Filling

¾ cup butter
1 tsp. vanilla
2½ cups powdered sugar
1 T. milk

DIRECTIONS

Preheat the oven to 375°F. In a stand mixer, cream the butter, both sugars, egg, vanilla, and molasses. In a separate large bowl, combine the flour, oats, salt, cinnamon, and baking soda. Slowly incorporate the dry and wet ingredients and mix until a soft dough forms. Line two large cookie sheets with parchment paper. Scoop about 2 ounces of dough (or a generous tablespoonful) and drop about 2 inches apart on the cookie sheet; gently press down. Place the cookie sheet in the refrigerator for about 10 minutes to prevent the dough from spreading in the oven. Bake the cookies for 10 to 12 minutes or until golden brown. Let cool. While the cookies are baking, prepare the filling: In a stand mixer, cream butter, vanilla, powdered sugar, and milk until smooth. When cookies have completely cooled, match them in pairs based on size. Pipe the filling into the center of one cookie and top with another cookie to form a cookie sandwich.

Let's be honest: Who doesn't love an oatmeal cream pie from a box? And aren't there some treats that you wish to have just one more bite? These oatmeal cream pies are BIGGER, and since I'm being honest, they are better than Little Debbie's! Shhhh, don't tell her. PIE-rrific for dessert, an afternoon treat, or any kiddo's lunch box!

TARA'S FAVORITE ICE CREAM PIE

PREP TIME: 3½ hours **YIELD:** 1 (9-inch) pie

INGREDIENTS

1 Chocolate Cornflake Crust (page 13)
1½ quarts ice cream—vanilla, chocolate, or coffee flavor
Fresh fruit, toasted nuts, or caramel sauce, optional

DIRECTIONS

Prepare or set out the Cornflake crust.

Press your favorite ice cream into the shell and freeze for 2 hours. Top with fresh fruit, nuts, or caramel sauce, if desired.

Growing up in the restaurant business, we met people around the table daily; through that, relationships began to grow, and a lasting community was built on a firm foundation. One of my most treasured relationships is with the Bolton family. Carol and Tim invited us to their table in Fredericksburg, Texas. One of our favorite meeting places was Peach Tree Inn, where we were introduced to their ice cream pie. This pie floods my memory with the sweet times we had together.

CAFÉ'S ORIGINAL BUTTERMILK PIE

PREP TIME: 15 minutes **BAKE TIME:** 55 minutes

YIELD: 1 (9-inch) pie

INGREDIENTS

1 (1 lb.) Royers dough ball (page 11) or 9-inch unbaked pie shell
½ cup butter
1⅔ cups plus 1 T. sugar
3 eggs
¼ cup flour
¾ cup plus 2 T. buttermilk
½ tsp. nutmeg
½ tsp. vanilla

DIRECTIONS

Preheat the oven to 325°F. Roll out the dough ball until it is ¼ inch thick and lay it in a 9-inch pie pan. Press dough into the base of the pie pan and crimp the edge with your two forefingers. In a stand mixer, cream the butter and sugar. Mix in the eggs and flour. Stir in the buttermilk, nutmeg, and vanilla. Pour filling into the unbaked pie shell. Bake for 55 minutes or until the filling is set and the crust is golden.

When our family took over the Round Top Cafe in 1987, there were only two pie flavors: buttermilk and apple. The buttermilk is still on the menu, and it was always my mom's favorite, especially served chilled.

BUTTERMILK DELIGHT PIE

PREP TIME: 15 minutes **BAKE TIME:** 55 minutes

YIELD: 1 (9-inch) pie

INGREDIENTS

1 (1 lb.) Royers dough ball (page 11) or 9-inch unbaked pie shell
½ cup butter
1⅔ cups plus 1 T. sugar
3 eggs
¼ cup flour
¾ cup plus 2 T. buttermilk
½ tsp. nutmeg
½ tsp. vanilla
1 cup chocolate chips
1 cup pecan pieces
1 cup unsweetened coconut flakes

DIRECTIONS

Preheat the oven to 325°F. Roll out the dough ball until it is ¼ inch thick and lay it in a 9-inch pie pan. Press dough into the base of the pie pan and crimp the edge with your two forefingers. In a stand mixer, cream the butter and sugar. Mix in the eggs and flour. Stir in the buttermilk, nutmeg, and vanilla and set aside.

In a separate bowl, combine chocolate chips, pecans, and coconut. Pour these dry ingredients into the bottom of the unbaked pie shell and then pour buttermilk filling over. Bake for 55 minutes or until the filling is set and the crust is golden.

One day my dad, Bud The Pieman, was in the kitchen making buttermilk pies when some chocolate chips fell into the filling. Instead of starting over, he added some coconut and pecan pieces, and voilà, Buttermilk Delight! This is my father-in-law's favorite pie, especially when warmed up. I personally like it chilled, haha!

RICK'S HAWT CHOCOLATE PIE

PREP TIME: 15 minutes **BAKE TIME:** 55 minutes

YIELD: 1 (9-inch) pie

INGREDIENTS

1 (1 lb.) Royers dough ball (page 11) or 9-inch unbaked pie shell
½ cup plus 2½ tsp. cocoa powder
1¾ cups plus 2½ tsp. sugar
Pinch of salt
¾ cup plus 2½ tsp. evaporated milk
3 eggs
1 T. orange zest
⅜ tsp. vanilla
⅕ of a habanero pepper, seeds removed, minced

DIRECTIONS

Preheat the oven to 325°F. Roll out the dough ball until it is ¼ inch thick and lay it in a 9-inch pie pan. Press dough into the base of the pie pan and crimp the edge with your two forefingers. In a stand mixer, combine cocoa, sugar, and salt. Add in wet ingredients and orange zest and mix well. Add in habanero (wear gloves when cutting!). Pour into the pie shell and bake for 55 minutes or until the filling is set and the crust is golden.

My husband, Rick, worked on this pie recipe for a long time. Initially, we called it The Spicy Rick, but he didn't like that, so we compromised with the Hawt Chocolate! It's a smooth chocolate chess pie with orange zest and a spicy kick on the back of the tongue. It is so delicious, especially chilled.

KEY LIME CHESS PIE

PREP TIME: 30 minutes **BAKE TIME:** 45 minutes

YIELD: 1 (9-inch) pie

INGREDIENTS

- 1 (1 lb.) Royers dough ball (page 11) or 9-inch unbaked pie shell
- ½ cup key lime juice (juice of 20 to 25 key limes)
- 4 eggs
- ¼ cup butter, melted
- ¼ cup flour
- 2 cups sugar
- 3 tsp. lime zest
- ¼ tsp. salt

DIRECTIONS

Preheat the oven to 325°F. Roll out the dough ball until it is ¼ inch thick and lay it in a 9-inch pie pan. Press dough into the base of the pie pan and crimp the edge with your two forefingers. In a mixing bowl, combine all ingredients and pour into an unbaked pie shell. Bake for 45 minutes or until the top is golden and a knife comes out clean.

This is not your typical key lime chess pie. We look at a few things when we create a new pie recipe. Are customers asking for it? Do we have the proper storage space? Is it shippable? And is it O.M.P. (Oh My Pie!)? We don't have storage or space for cream-type pies, but we think you'll love this pie.

SAM'S COCONUT LEMON CHESS PIE

PREP TIME: 15 minutes **BAKE TIME:** 60 minutes

YIELD: 1 (9-inch) pie

INGREDIENTS

1 (1 lb.) Royers dough ball (page 11) or 9-inch unbaked pie shell
¼ cup flour
1⅔ cups sugar
Pinch of salt
3 T. butter, melted
4 eggs
2 T. lemon zest
⅔ cup lemon juice
1 T. vanilla
2 cups unsweetened coconut flakes

DIRECTIONS

Preheat the oven to 325°F. Roll out the dough ball until it is ¼ inch thick and lay it in a 9-inch pie pan. Press dough into the base of the pie pan and crimp the edge with your two forefingers. Combine all ingredients in a bowl, mix well, and pour into the pie shell. Bake for 60 minutes or until the crust is golden.

Sam Robinson worked with us from an early age. We also attended school together. He began washing dishes but quickly learned all the skills needed to run a café. Sam was a hard worker and said he was going to be president. One night, he fell asleep at the wheel and passed away. He is greatly missed; he would have been one heck of a president! This is a Tara-rized version of a recipe he created many years ago.

BLUEBERRY LEMON PIE

PREP TIME: 45 minutes **BAKE TIME:** 45 minutes

YIELD: 1 (9-inch) pie

INGREDIENTS

1 (1 lb.) Royers dough ball (page 11) or 9-inch unbaked pie shell

Blueberry Filling

½ cup flour
1 cup water
4 cups blueberries, fresh or frozen
1¼ cups sugar
¼ cup lemon juice

Lemon Cream Cheese Filling

8 oz. cream cheese, softened
½ cup powdered sugar
1 tsp. vanilla
1 T. lemon juice
1 egg
½ cup flour
1 tsp. lemon zest

Crumble Topping

1 cup brown sugar
¾ tsp. cinnamon
1 cup old-fashioned oats
½ cup flour
⅛ tsp. salt
Pinch of nutmeg
½ cup butter, melted

DIRECTIONS

Preheat the oven to 325°F. Roll out the dough ball until it is ¼ inch thick and lay it in a 9-inch pie pan. Press dough into the base of the pie pan and crimp the edge with your two forefingers.

For the blueberry filling, combine the flour and water in a small bowl, whisk until combined, and set aside. Pour the blueberries, sugar, and lemon juice into a braising pot and stir over medium heat until it begins to boil. Add the flour and water mixture and stir until the sauce thickens, a good 5 minutes. Remove from heat. In a stand mixer (or a bowl and good ole hand mixer), add all ingredients for the lemon cream cheese filling and whip until smooth. Next up is the crumble topping. Mix the dry ingredients together in a bowl until combined. Add the butter until mixture crumbles in your hands.

To assemble, spread half of the blueberry filling on the bottom of the pie crust, then spread the lemon cream cheese filling over the blueberries. Add the remaining blueberry filling to the top of the lemon cream cheese and top with crumble topping. Bake for 45 minutes or until the topping is golden brown.

Blueberry Lemon is one of those pies that has evolved over the years. It began with a simple lattice crust, and through the years my love for experimenting grew as I learned more about pies, fillings, toppings, and what flavors pair well together. Blueberry Lemon is one of my favorite combinations.

JUNKBERRY PIE

PREP TIME: 45 minutes **BAKE TIME:** 45 minutes

YIELD: 1 (9-inch) pie

INGREDIENTS

1 (1 lb.) Royers dough ball (page 11) or 9-inch unbaked pie shell

Junkberry Filling

1 Granny Smith apple
1½ cups peaches, fresh or frozen
1 cup strawberries, fresh or frozen
1 cup blueberries, fresh or frozen
1 cup blackberries, fresh or frozen
½ cup raspberries, fresh or frozen
¾ cup sugar
½ cup flour

Junkberry Topping

½ cup sour cream
¼ tsp. salt
½ cup flour
⅔ cup sugar, plus extra for sprinkling

DIRECTIONS

Preheat the oven to 325°F. Roll out the dough ball until it is ¼ inch thick and lay it in a 9-inch pie pan. Press dough into the base of the pie pan and crimp the edge with your two forefingers. Peel and core the apple and slice it into 8 pieces. Combine peaches and strawberries in a large sauté pan and heat for 2 to 3 minutes on medium. Add remaining fruit and sugar and heat until sugar forms a syrup, stirring often. Add in flour and stir until all combined. Pour the filling into the pie shell; the fruit does not have to be thoroughly cooked because it will continue baking in the oven.

To make the topping, combine the ingredients in a medium bowl, spread evenly over the fruit filling, and sprinkle with extra sugar. Bake for 45 minutes. Let cool until the filling is set.

I had been in the kitchen making different pies and had some leftover fruit, but I needed more to make individual pies. So, I thought, throw in all the "junk" left over and make a mixed-berry pie. Being from Round Top, we are known for our "junkin'" antique shows, and it only seemed fitting to name it Junkberry Pie.

I use lots of frozen fruit because life happens, and sometimes the fresh fruit I bought to make an item goes bad before I get around to baking it. Frozen fruit doesn't spoil, and it's fresh fruit—just frozen!

NOT MY MOM'S APPLE PIE

PREP TIME: 30 minutes **BAKE TIME:** 60 minutes

YIELD: 1 (9-inch) pie

INGREDIENTS

1 (1 lb.) Royers dough ball (page 11) or 9-inch unbaked pie shell
6 to 7 medium Granny Smith apples

Filling

1⅓ cups packed brown sugar
⅔ cup heavy whipping cream
¼ cup flour

Streusel Topping

1 cup brown sugar
½ cup pecan pieces
3 T. flour
2 tsp. cinnamon
2 tsp. butter, melted

DIRECTIONS

Preheat the oven to 325°F. Roll out the dough ball until it is ¼ inch thick and lay it in a 9-inch pie pan. Press dough into the base of the pie pan and crimp the edge with your two forefingers. Peel, core, and cut the apples into quarters. Layer the apple pieces in the unbaked pie crust. Mix the brown sugar, whipping cream, and flour. Pour the filling over the apples.

In a separate bowl, mix the brown sugar, pecans, flour, and cinnamon, and then stir in the melted butter. Press the topping over the apples to form a dome. Bake for 60 minutes or until the filling bubbles through the topping.

One day, my nana (my dad's mom) came to visit, and of course, after lunch, she had to have pie. She tried our apple pie and exclaimed, "This is not my pie!" My dad quickly replied, "No, it's not!" Obviously, we had to change the name to Not My Mom's Apple Pie.

PEACHY KEEN PIE

PREP TIME: 20 minutes **BAKE TIME:** 45 minutes

YIELD: 1 (9-inch) pie

INGREDIENTS

1 (1 lb.) Royers dough ball (page 11) or 9-inch unbaked pie shell

Peach Filling

8 cups peaches, fresh or frozen

1 cup sugar

¼ cup cornstarch

Crumble Topping

1¼ cups yellow cake mix

9 T. brown sugar

1⅓ tsp. cinnamon

3 T. butter, melted

DIRECTIONS

Preheat the oven to 325°F. Roll out the dough ball until it is ¼ inch thick and lay it in a 9-inch pie pan. Press dough into the base of the pie pan and crimp the edge with your two forefingers. Add peaches to a large saucepan and heat on medium heat. Once the peaches soften and the juices bubble, add sugar and stir until it is dissolved. Add cornstarch and stir until thickened. Peaches don't need to be cooked down; whole peaches are what you want and will keep cooking in the oven. Pour peaches into the pie crust. Combine cake mix, brown sugar, cinnamon, and butter in a separate bowl. Sprinkle topping over the peaches. Bake for 45 minutes or until the topping is golden.

I love this pie. It is a bit sweet, but nothing a little ice cream can't cut! I use frozen peaches in my peach pie because I love their firmness and size. When frozen, they won't go bad and are always available when I want to bake up a refreshing pie.

PEANUT BUTTER RASPBERRY PIE

PREP TIME: 30 minutes **BAKE TIME:** 45 minutes

YIELD: 1 (9-inch) pie

INGREDIENTS

1 (1 lb.) Royers dough ball (page 11) or 9-inch unbaked pie shell

Raspberry Filling

3 cups raspberries, fresh or frozen
¾ cup sugar
3 tsp. lemon juice
3 tsp. vanilla
3 T. cornstarch

Peanut Butter Crumble Topping

1½ cups old-fashioned oats
¾ cup brown sugar
¼ cup sugar
½ cup flour
Pinch of salt
6 T. butter, softened
¼ cup creamy peanut butter, warmed

DIRECTIONS

Preheat the oven to 325°F. Roll out the dough ball until it is ¼ inch thick and lay it in a 9-inch pie pan. Press dough into the base of the pie pan and crimp the edge with your two forefingers. In a medium saucepan, add the raspberries and cook on medium heat until the fruit begins to break down; mix in the sugar, lemon juice, and vanilla. Once this is mixed well, add cornstarch and stir constantly so the fruit doesn't burn. Once thickened, set aside. Combine the oats, brown sugar, sugar, flour, salt, butter, and peanut butter in a separate bowl. Spoon raspberry filling into the pie shell and cover with crumble topping. Bake for 45 minutes.

When I create, I love to make something that I know the boys will love. Brayden is open to trying new things and usually loves any of my experiments. Bentley is a hard sell, but I'll keep working on him! When I met Rick, he didn't eat dessert. Now he loves dessert. Oops! This is one of his favorites.

Don't forget that every oven is different, so cooking times and temperatures will always vary. You know your oven. It's better to set a timer to check your item 15 minutes before the suggested time. If it's not done, just add more time. You can't unburn an item, ha!

RASPBERRY LEMON PIE

PREP TIME: 15 minutes **BAKE TIME:** 60 minutes

YIELD: 1 (9-inch) pie

INGREDIENTS

1 (1 lb.) Royers dough ball (page 11) or 9-inch unbaked pie shell

Raspberry Filling

1¼ cups raspberries, fresh or frozen
¼ cup sugar
1 tsp. lemon juice
1 tsp. vanilla
1 T. cornstarch

Lemon Filling

6 T. flour
1⅔ cups sugar
Pinch of salt
3 T. butter, melted
4 eggs
2 T. lemon zest
⅔ cup lemon juice
1 T. vanilla

DIRECTIONS

Preheat the oven to 275°F. Roll out the dough ball until it is ¼ inch thick and lay it in a 9-inch pie pan. Press dough into the base of the pie pan and crimp the edge with your two forefingers. Add the raspberries, sugar, lemon juice, and vanilla to a small saucepan over medium heat. Bring to a simmer, add in cornstarch, and stir until mixture thickens. Remove from heat and pour into the bottom of the unbaked pie shell. Combine the flour, sugar, salt, butter, eggs, lemon zest, lemon juice, and vanilla in a separate bowl. Pour onto raspberry filling and bake for 60 minutes. Chill before serving and sprinkle with powdered sugar.

Raspberry Lemon Pie . . . Jump for joy! You could probably do so many jumps for joy when you eat this pie, it would cancel out the calories. The PIE-fect amount of sweet and tart baked in a pie shell; wonderful when chilled or even eaten right out of the freezer. Take it to any family picnic, and you will be the life of the party!

CHERRY PIE

PREP TIME: 15 minutes **BAKE TIME:** 45 minutes
YIELD: 1 (9-inch) pie

This pie has a secret ingredient you may be shocked to hear about! There is something about cherry filling out of a can; it's simple and nostalgic. So, are you shocked that we use canned cherries at Royers Pie Haven? I was chatting with our team one afternoon and asked, "What do you think about making our own cherry filling?" Quickly they responded with, "Why mess up a good thing?" Sometimes we need an easy pie to throw into the oven for an impromptu gathering of friends and family.

INGREDIENTS

2 (1 lb.) Royers dough balls (page 11) or 2 (9-inch) unbaked pie shells
2 (21 oz.) cans cherry pie filling
Butter, melted
Cinnamon for sprinkling
Sugar for sprinkling

DIRECTIONS

Preheat the oven to 325°F. Roll out one dough ball until it is ¼ inch thick and lay it in the 9-inch pie pan. Press dough into the base of the pie pan and crimp the edge with your two forefingers. Pour the cherries into the pie crust. Using a portion of the other prepared dough ball, sprinkle the counter with flour and roll the dough into a circle about ¼ inch thick. Cut dough into strips and basket weave the dough on the cherry filling. Brush with melted butter and sprinkle with cinnamon and sugar. Bake for 45 minutes, until the crust is golden and the cherries are bubbling.

SUGAR-FREE PEACH PIE

PREP TIME: 15 minutes **BAKE TIME:** 45 minutes

YIELD: 1 (9-inch) pie

INGREDIENTS

- 2 (1 lb.) Royers dough balls (page 11) or 2 (9-inch) unbaked pie shells
- 8 cups peaches, fresh or frozen
- 12 Equal packets (or favorite sugar substitute), plus an extra for topping
- 3 T. cornstarch
- Butter, melted
- Cinnamon

DIRECTIONS

Preheat the oven to 325°F. Roll out one of the dough balls until it is ¼ inch thick and lay it in the 9-inch pie pan. Press dough into the base of the pie pan and crimp the edge with your two forefingers. Add peaches to a large saucepan and cook over medium heat. Once the peaches soften and the juices bubble, add Equal and stir until totally dissolved. Add cornstarch and stir until thickened. Peaches don't need to be cooked down; whole peach chunks are what you want and will keep cooking in the oven. Pour peach mixture into the pie crust.

Using a portion of the second dough ball, sprinkle the counter with flour and roll the dough into a circle about ¼ inch thick. Cut dough into strips and basket weave the dough on top of the peach filling. Brush with melted butter and sprinkle with cinnamon and Equal. Bake for 45 minutes, until the crust is golden and the peaches are bubbling.

Being a pie shop, everyone comes in for pie, but some can't have "real" pie. Ha! We always love to see a need and find a solution. Adding sugar-free pie was easy! It's simple, and you wouldn't know it's sugar-free unless you asked. This pie gives all the freshness of peaches and a little sugar alternative to bring joy to everyone at the table.

D'ETTE'S STRAWBERRY RHUBARB PIE

PREP TIME: 30 minutes **BAKE TIME:** 45 minutes

YIELD: 1 (9-inch) pie

INGREDIENTS

1 (1 lb.) Royers dough ball (page 11) or 9-inch unbaked pie shell

Strawberry Rhubarb Filling

4 cups rhubarb, fresh or frozen, cut into pieces
3 cups strawberries, fresh or frozen
1 cup sugar
½ cup flour
2 T. butter
1½ tsp. lemon juice

Crumble Topping

1 cup brown sugar
¾ tsp. cinnamon
1 cup old-fashioned oats
½ cup flour
⅛ tsp. salt
Pinch of nutmeg
½ cup butter, melted

DIRECTIONS

Preheat the oven to 325°F. Roll out the dough ball until it is ¼ inch thick and lay it in a 9-inch pie pan. Press dough into the base of the pie pan and crimp the edge with your two forefingers. Pour the rhubarb, strawberries, sugar, flour, butter, and lemon juice into a braising pot and stir over medium heat until it begins to boil and thicken. Stir constantly so the bottom doesn't burn. Turn off heat. Next up is the crumble topping. Add the dry ingredients together in a bowl and mix until combined. Add the butter to the dry ingredients and mix until it crumbles in your hands. Scoop the fruit filling into the pie crust and press crumble topping on the filling to cover the whole pie. Bake for 45 minutes or until the topping is golden brown.

Usually a pie is named after someone because it's a pie they created, but this one we named after a customer's fond love for it! D'ette would come to eat at the café every Texas Antiques Week and always had to have her strawberry rhubarb pie! Rhubarb looks like celery and grows up north. It's very tart, but the strawberries' sweetness (and lots of SUGAH) makes it a PIE-fect combination.

JOY

COFFEE JOY PIE

NUT PIES

PREP TIME: 10 minutes **BAKE TIME:** 45 minutes

YIELD: 1 (9-inch) pie

INGREDIENTS

1 (1 lb.) Royers dough ball (page 11) or 9-inch unbaked pie shell
3 cups shredded coconut
½ cup chocolate chips
1 cup sliced almonds
½ cup butter
2 T. espresso powder
1 (14 oz.) can sweetened condensed milk

DIRECTIONS

Preheat the oven to 325°F. Roll out the dough ball until it is ¼ inch thick and lay it in a 9-inch pie pan. Press dough into the base of the pie pan and crimp the edge with your two forefingers. Combine all ingredients in a bowl and toss into your pie crust. Bake for 45 minutes. Let cool before serving.

I'm not one to pick a pie that has coconut in it, but this pie has changed my perspective. This is my take on an Almond Joy candy bar with coffee. It's PIE-fect with a cup of coffee and a toothpick on the side.

ANN'S PECAN PIE

PREP TIME: 15 minutes **BAKE TIME:** 35 to 45 minutes

YIELD: 1 (9-inch) pie

INGREDIENTS

1 (1 lb.) Royers dough ball (page 11) or 9-inch unbaked pie shell
⅓ cup butter, melted
1 cup sugar
1 cup light corn syrup
1 tsp. vanilla
1 tsp. salt
4 eggs
1½ cups pecan halves

DIRECTIONS

Preheat the oven to 325°F. Roll out the dough ball until it is ¼ inch thick and lay it in a 9-inch pie pan. Press dough into the base of the pie pan and crimp the edge with your two forefingers. Stir the butter, sugar, corn syrup, vanilla, and salt in a medium mixing bowl until combined. Add in the eggs and mix well. Pour filling into your pie crust and cover it with pecan halves. Bake for 45 minutes or until bubbly and the crust is golden. You can also test it with a knife, which should come out clean. Let the pie cool for at least 30 minutes, and top it with your favorite vanilla ice cream.

When our family took over the Round Top Cafe, my parents worked hard to build relationships. One was with Ann Criswell of the *Houston Chronicle*. Ann was the food editor and knew we didn't have a pecan pie recipe. She shared her recipe with us over 30 years ago. It's not too sweet, just right.

Baking by sight and smell is the best way! If you are aware, you will notice that the aroma becomes more profound as your recipe cooks. And if the crust looks nice and golden, you know you are getting close!

MO' PIE U BOURBON CHOCOLATE PECAN PIE

PREP TIME: 30 minutes **BAKE TIME:** 76 minutes

YIELD: 1 (9-inch) pie

INGREDIENTS

1 (1 lb.) Royers dough ball (page 11) or 9-inch unbaked pie shell
⅔ cup chocolate chips
1½ cups pecan halves
1 cup sugar
¼ tsp. salt
1 tsp. vanilla
4 eggs
½ cup butter, melted
1 cup plus 1 T. light corn syrup
2 oz. bourbon

DIRECTIONS

Preheat the oven to 375°F. Roll out the dough ball until it is ¼ inch thick and lay it in a 9-inch pie pan. Press dough into the base of the pie pan and crimp the edge with your two forefingers. Spread the chocolate chips and pecans evenly in the bottom of the shell. Using an electric mixer, combine the sugar, salt, and vanilla in a medium bowl. Add in the eggs and mix well. Next, add the butter and mix until smooth. Finally, add in the corn syrup and bourbon, pouring them in slowly while the mixer is on low speed. When the filling is mixed well, pour it over the chocolate chips and pecans in the pie shell. Bake for 12 minutes, then turn down to 275°F and bake an additional 64 minutes or until bubbly and the crust is golden. You can also test it with a knife, which should come out clean. Allow to cool for 30 minutes before eating or freezing.

Our friend Mark Devlin founded Mo Pie U, a nonprofit organization established to provide college tuition support and make a difference in the lives of children who have lost a parent to cancer. We met Mark when he was on a weekend getaway to Round Top with his wife. He was looking for a bakery to bake his Bourbon Chocolate Pecan Pie for his nonprofit. The owner of the bed and breakfast he was staying at told him to go to Round Top and visit Royers Pie Haven. He took them up on their advice, and when he walked into Royers Pie Haven, he saw a quote on our pie box, "Eat Mo' Pie." That was the beginning of a PIE-rrific relationship, and as they say, "the rest is history!" Visit mopieu.org to learn more.

JB'S WHITE CHOCOLATE MACADAMIA NUT PIE

PREP TIME: 10 minutes **BAKE TIME:** 40 minutes

YIELD: 1 (9-inch) pie

INGREDIENTS

- 1 (1 lb.) Royers dough ball (page 11) or 9-inch unbaked pie shell
- 2 eggs
- 9 T. brown sugar
- 6 T. dark corn syrup
- 3 T. butter, melted
- 2¼ tsp. vanilla
- 9 T. flour
- ½ cup macadamia nuts, whole
- ¼ cup shredded coconut
- ¾ cup white chocolate chips

This is one of my brother JB's recipes. JB and his wife, Jamie-Len, are the latest owners of our family business, Royers Round Top Cafe. I love this pie. It's got a great caramel flavor, and the whole macadamia nuts give it a wonderful crunch.

DIRECTIONS

Preheat the oven to 325°F. Roll out the dough ball until it is ¼ inch thick and lay it in a 9-inch pie pan. Press dough into the base of the pie pan and crimp the edge with your two forefingers. In a large bowl, whisk the eggs until they are frothy. Stir in the brown sugar, corn syrup, butter, and vanilla until combined. Fold in the flour, then add in nuts, coconut, and white chocolate chips. Pour into the pie shell and bake for 40 minutes until the crust is golden and a knife comes clean.

SUGAR-FREE PECAN PIE

PREP TIME: 10 minutes **BAKE TIME:** 45 minutes

YIELD: 1 (9-inch) pie

INGREDIENTS

1 (1 lb.) Royers dough ball (page 11) or 9-inch unbaked pie shell
¼ cup butter, melted
⅔ cup Splenda
1⅓ cups HoneyTree sugar-free honey
2½ tsp. vanilla
5 eggs
¼ cup flour
Pinch of salt
1½ cups pecan pieces

DIRECTIONS

Preheat the oven to 325°F. Roll out the dough ball until it is ¼ inch thick and lay it in a 9-inch pie pan. Press dough into the base of the pie pan and crimp the edge with your two forefingers. Mix butter, Splenda, honey, vanilla, eggs, flour, and salt in a large bowl. Pour into the unbaked pie shell and top with pecan pieces. Bake for 45 minutes or until the filling is bubbly.

This recipe was passed down from our precious friend Mrs. Wilson. Sugar-free honey is a beautiful sugar substitute; many people love this pie more than our regular pecan pie. You're probably wondering how you make sugar-free honey? Me too, but it works. Trust the process.

PiES

SAVORY PIES

{A Dollop of Comfort}

Savory quickly reminds me of the scripture, "Taste and see that the Lord is good. How happy is the person who takes refuge in him!" Psalm 34:8 (CSB). I mentioned in the introduction that my dad taught me about depth in flavor. When my brothers and I would create a new menu item, we made sure you could taste the depth on the back of your tongue. We would take the latest creation to Dad to try, and sometimes he said, "Needs more depth!" We would return to the kitchen and persevere to get the best flavor humanly possible. It reminds me of life with God: We keep sitting with Him to be seasoned with salt, so when we share a meal around the table, our conversations go deep below the surface to illuminate Him and us. Colossians 4:6 says, "Let your speech always be gracious, seasoned with salt, so that you may know how you should answer each person." We added savory pies to the menu at Royers Pie Haven as our answer to customers desiring more than a slice of sweet pie, a sandwich, or a salad. If you come to the Haven now, you can get a sweet 'n' savory combo and add a pie shake for your drink! (Pie shake is extra, of course! Ha!) Three slices of pie for lunch? Yes, please!

MISSISSIPPI POT ROAST PIE

BEEF PIES

PREP TIME: 9 hours **BAKE TIME:** 45 minutes

YIELD: 1 (9-inch) pie

INGREDIENTS

1 (1 lb.) Royers herb dough ball (page 12) or 9-inch unbaked pie shell

Mississippi Pot Roast

2 to 2½ lbs. chuck roast
1 (1 oz.) pkg. ranch seasoning mix
¼ cup water
1 (10 oz.) pkg. au jus gravy mix
3 to 4 whole pepperoncini peppers

Mashed Potatoes

2 lbs. russet potatoes, cut into large chunks
1 cup sour cream
1 (1 oz.) pkg. ranch seasoning mix
Salt and pepper

DIRECTIONS

Place the chuck roast, ranch seasoning mix, water, au jus gravy mix, and peppers in your Crock-Pot and cook on low for 8 hours. An hour before your roast is done, roll out the dough ball until it is ¼ inch thick and lay it in a 9-inch pie pan. Press dough into the base of the pie pan and crimp the edge with your two forefingers. Fill a large pot with water, add the potatoes, and boil. When potatoes are tender, drain water and mash. Stir the sour cream and ranch seasoning mix into the potatoes until combined, and set aside. Preheat the oven to 325°F.

When the roast is done, remove it from the Crock-Pot and place it on a cutting board to remove any excess juice. Shred roast into bite-size pieces and add to your unbaked pie shell. You can chop and add the pepperoncini to the pie or discard them if you prefer. Top with mashed potatoes and sprinkle with salt and pepper. Bake for 45 minutes.

We make this as a casserole for the Bake Shop or fundraisers, but added it recently to our fall menu at Royers Pie Haven. It is hearty, and the depth of flavor is O.M.P.

PEPPERONI PIZZA PIE

PREP TIME: 30 minutes **BAKE TIME:** 45 minutes

YIELD: 1 (9-inch) pie

During COVID, we had to shift our focus because pie alone would not get us by! We stood in the Bake Shop kitchen with our two team members and asked for divine direction. God quickly answered, and in 24 hours, we had a plan. We had a freezer full of over 2,500 savory and sweet pies because we were ready for Texas Antiques Week, and the local county officials had just canceled it. We started a Facebook group called "Feed His People" and offered door-dropping dinner and dessert because we had the space, staff that needed a job, food deliveries from our suppliers, and affordable prices. For months, we delivered to over 75 different families weekly. This pie was created for all those kiddos who just wanted a pepperoni pizza during COVID.

INGREDIENTS

- 1 (1 lb.) Royers herb dough ball (page 12) or 9-inch unbaked pie shell
- 1 cup breakfast sausage (about 8 oz.)
- 2 T. butter
- 1 cup cherry tomatoes, halved
- ½ cup diced red onion
- 1 tsp. chopped garlic
- ¼ tsp. Louise's Herb Mix (page 12)
- Pinch of red chili flakes
- 1 cup grated Parmesan
- 1 cup shredded mozzarella
- 1 cup fresh mozzarella, torn into pieces
- 1 cup marinara
- ¼ cup fresh basil, chopped
- 8 oz. sliced pepperoni

DIRECTIONS

Preheat the oven to 325°F. Roll out the dough ball until it is ¼ inch thick and lay it in a 9-inch pie pan. Press dough into the base of the pie pan and crimp the edge with your two forefingers. In a medium skillet, brown the sausage a bit, and then stir in the butter, and add the cherry tomatoes, red onion, garlic, herb mix, and chili flakes. Sauté until sausage is cooked through and set aside.

Combine the Parmesan, shredded mozzarella, fresh mozzarella, marinara, and basil in a large mixing bowl. Add in the cooked sausage mixture. Layer one-third of the sausage and cheese mixture on the bottom of the pie crust, then add a layer of one-third of the pepperoni. Layer twice more until all the filling and pepperoni are added. Bake for 45 minutes.

SOUTHWEST TACO PIE

PREP TIME: 20 minutes **BAKE TIME:** 45 minutes

YIELD: 1 (9-inch) pie

INGREDIENTS

2 (1 lb.) Royers dough balls (page 11) or 2 (9-inch) unbaked pie shells
2 cups ground beef
1 (1.25 oz.) pkg. taco seasoning mix
1 cup favorite salsa
1 cup corn, fresh, frozen, or canned
1 cup black or pinto beans, drained
1 cup shredded cheddar cheese
1 (4 oz.) can of green chiles
Butter, melted

DIRECTIONS

Preheat the oven to 325°F. Roll out one dough ball until it is ¼ inch thick and lay it in a 9-inch pie pan. Press dough into the base of the pie pan. In a skillet, brown the beef and add taco seasoning, setting aside a bit of the seasoning to sprinkle on the top. Set beef aside to cool. Mix the salsa, corn, beans, cheese, and green chiles in a large bowl until combined. Add the taco meat, mix thoroughly, then add to the pie shell and spread to fill.

Roll out the second ball of pie dough until it is ¼ inch thick, and carefully place it on top of the taco mixture, then crimp the edges with your two forefingers to seal the pie. Brush the crust with butter and sprinkle with the remaining taco seasoning. Bake for 45 minutes or until the top of the pie is golden brown. Remove from the oven and cool before serving.

I'm sure you've heard of Taco Tuesday, but have you ever had Taco Tuesday PIE style? You might never be able to return to regular tacos again; just sayin'. Feel free to add your favorite taco toppings on top too!

SHEPHERD'S PIE

PREP TIME: 45 minutes **BAKE TIME:** 45 minutes

YIELD: 1 (9-inch) pie

INGREDIENTS

1 (1 lb.) Royers herb dough ball (page 12) or 9-inch unbaked pie shell
2 lbs. russet potatoes, cut into large chunks
1½ lbs. ground lamb or beef
1¾ tsp. lemon pepper
1 tsp. garlic powder
¼ tsp. salt
1 cup sour cream
1 (1 oz.) pkg. ranch seasoning mix
2 cups frozen mixed vegetables
⅔ cup diced red onion
3 tsp. fresh rosemary, chopped
½ cup shredded cheddar

DIRECTIONS

Preheat the oven to 325°F. Roll out the dough ball until it is ¼ inch thick and lay it in a 9-inch pie pan. Press dough into the base of the pie pan and crimp the edge with your two forefingers. Fill a large pot with water, add potatoes, and bring to a boil. Meanwhile, in a large sauté pan, brown the ground meat, lemon pepper, garlic powder, and salt.

When potatoes are tender, drain water and mash. Stir the sour cream and ranch seasoning mix into the potatoes until combined and set aside. In a separate bowl, combine the vegetables, onion, and rosemary.

Now, let's layer our pie! Fill the bottom of the unbaked pie shell with the vegetable mixture, add the meat mixture, and top with mashed potatoes. Bake the pie for 45 minutes. Sprinkle with cheddar and enjoy!

This pie is Rick's favorite. It's meat and potatoes all mashed together. Now, if you don't like your food touching, this might not be the pie for you, haha! I did a little digging into the origin of shepherd's pie and learned it was named after the shepherds who herded their sheep. I told Rick about it, and he said, "I love that my favorite pie is about my Shepherd and His lamb."

BBQ CHICKEN PIZZA PIE

PREP TIME: 30 minutes **BAKE TIME:** 45 minutes

YIELD: 1 (9-inch) pie

INGREDIENTS

2 (1 lb.) Royers herb dough balls (page 12) or 2 (9-inch) unbaked pie shells
1 T. olive oil
1½ lbs. chicken breast, cubed
1 tsp. salt
1 tsp. black pepper
1 tsp. Season-All (find on any grocery store spice row)
1 medium red onion, sliced
2 T. chopped garlic
1 cup fresh cilantro, chopped
1 cup favorite barbecue sauce
½ cup honey
1 cup shredded cheddar
5 slices Swiss cheese
Butter

DIRECTIONS

Preheat the oven to 325°F. Roll out one dough ball until it is ¼ inch thick and lay it in a 9-inch pie pan. Press the dough into the base of the pie pan and set aside. In a large skillet, heat the olive oil and then add the chicken with the salt, pepper, and Season-All. Sauté for about 10 minutes, then add the onion, garlic, and cilantro. Continue sautéing until the onions are translucent. Add the barbecue sauce, bring to a boil, then add the honey, cheddar, and Swiss. Pour the mixture into your unbaked pie crust. Roll out the other dough ball until it is ¼ inch thick and place it on top of the pie. Crimp edges with two forefingers, brush the top with butter, and bake for 45 minutes.

This reci-PIE is inspired by our love for pizza and our favorite flavor, BBQ chicken. Take what you love, use what you have, and put your creative spin on it. This pie would be excellent with a potato salad, a big ole bowl of Caesar salad, and Tara's Chocolate Chip Cookies. A PIE-fect family picnic!

CHICKEN MARGHERITA PIE

PREP TIME: 30 minutes **BAKE TIME:** 60 minutes

YIELD: 1 (9-inch) pie

INGREDIENTS

1 (1 lb.) Royers herb dough ball (page 12) or 9-inch unbaked pie shell
1½ cups cubed fresh chicken breast
1 T. olive oil
½ yellow onion, chopped
1 T. chopped garlic
1½ cups shredded mozzarella
1 cup fresh mozzarella, torn into pieces
1 cup grated Parmesan
½ cup mayonnaise
3 T. chopped fresh basil, divided
2 tomatoes, sliced
Salt
Pepper

DIRECTIONS

Preheat the oven to 325°F. Roll out the dough ball until it is ¼ inch thick and lay it in a 9-inch pie pan. Press dough into the base of the pie pan and crimp the edge with your two forefingers. Heat water in a pot and boil the chicken cubes until no pink remains. In a sauté pan over medium heat, warm the olive oil and sauté the onion and garlic until they are transparent. Turn off the heat.

In a large mixing bowl, combine all the cheeses and the mayonnaise with the chicken, sautéed onion and garlic, and 2 tablespoons of the fresh basil. Layer half of the tomatoes in the bottom of the pie shell, then half of the chicken and cheese mixture, then repeat both layers. Sprinkle with reserved basil, and add salt and pepper to taste. Bake for 60 minutes or until the cheese is melted and golden. Let rest for 1 hour before serving. Enjoy!

My dad shared this recipe with me when we opened Royers Pie Haven in 2011. This pie is the GOAT! (Can you tell I have teenage boys?) But in all seriousness, this recipe launched our creative inspiration for savory reci-PIES. It's the pie that started it all.

CHICKEN, PIMIENTO, AND FETA PIE

PREP TIME: 30 minutes **BAKE TIME:** 45 minutes

YIELD: 1 (9-inch) pie

INGREDIENTS

1 (1 lb.) Royers herb dough ball (page 12) or 9-inch unbaked pie shell
1½ cups cubed fresh chicken breasts
2 cups shredded cheddar cheese
½ cup feta cheese
1 tsp. Mrs. Dash
½ cup mayonnaise
2 tsp. mustard

DIRECTIONS

Preheat the oven to 325°F. Roll out the dough ball until it is ¼ inch thick and lay it in a 9-inch pie pan. Press dough into the base of the pie pan and crimp the edge with your two forefingers. Heat water in a pot and boil the chicken cubes until no pink remains. Combine the cheddar, feta, Mrs. Dash, mayonnaise, mustard, and cooked chicken. Pour the mixture into your unbaked pie dough. Bake for 45 minutes or until the cheese is bubbly.

Pimiento cheese is often called "the caviar of the South." I'm not a fan of caviar, and I'm so glad that cheese, chicken, and herbs are what we consider fancy! Now, if you have only experienced a pimiento cheese sandwich from a convenience store, don't give up on this reci-PIE; it's out of this world! Maybe serve with a side of bacon, just sayin'. My husband loves to add a little jalapeño or cayenne.

Life is too short. If you mess up, it's just flour, sugar, and water. Start over.

CHICKEN POT PIE

PREP TIME: 45 minutes **BAKE TIME:** 45 minutes

YIELD: 1 (9-inch) pie

INGREDIENTS

2 (1 lb.) Royers herb dough balls (page 12) or 2 (9-inch) unbaked pie shells
3½ cups cubed fresh chicken breasts
½ cup diced yellow onion
½ T. chopped garlic
½ tsp. fresh rosemary, chopped
½ tsp. Season-All (in any grocery spice section)
¼ tsp. black pepper
¼ cup dill butter (recipe below)
¼ cup flour
½ cup heavy whipping cream
1½ cups chicken broth
¼ cup Parmesan cheese
1 cup mixed vegetables
Butter, melted
Mrs. Dash

DIRECTIONS

Preheat the oven to 325°F. Roll out one of the dough balls until it is ¼ inch thick and lay it in a 9-inch pie pan. Press dough into the base of the pie pan and set aside. Roll out the other dough ball to a ¼-inch thickness to cover the top of the pie and set aside. Heat water in a pot and boil the chicken cubes until no pink remains.

In a large skillet over medium heat, combine the dill butter, onion, garlic, rosemary, Season-All, and black pepper. Sauté until it bubbles. Then stir in the flour, cream, broth, and Parmesan until combined and thickened. Add in the cooked chicken and vegetables. Pour the mixture into the pie shell and cover with the top crust. Crimp the top with the pie crust edges, butter it, and sprinkle it with Mrs. Dash. Bake for 45 minutes.

I grew up loving a Stouffer's chicken pot pie on a cold, rainy day, and it was a quick and easy dinner. I love to keep a few of these in the freezer to take to someone who just had a baby, a new neighbor, or who experienced the loss of a friend or family member. Bake a sweet pie, and you will have a PIE-fect combo. As Craig Claiborne says, "There is nothing better on a cold wintry day than a properly made pot pie." I think he's got that right!

DILL BUTTER

YIELD: 2 cups

INGREDIENTS

1 chicken bouillon cube
1 T. water
1 lb. butter, softened
2 tsp. dill weed
1 tsp. chopped garlic
¼ cup white onion, diced

DIRECTIONS

Place the chicken bouillon cube and water in a bowl and microwave for one minute. Stir until dissolved. Place the butter in a mixing bowl and add the bouillon mix, dill weed, garlic, and onion, and mix well. Store in an air-tight container in the refrigerator.

GREEN CHILE CHICKEN PIE

PREP TIME: 15 minutes **BAKE TIME:** 35 to 45 minutes

YIELD: 1 (9-inch) pie

INGREDIENTS

- 2 (1 lb.) Royers herb dough balls (page 12) or 2 (9-inch) unbaked pie shells
- 3 cups cubed fresh chicken breasts
- 1 cup salsa verde or avocado salsa
- 1 cup shredded pepper jack cheese
- 1 (4 oz.) can green chiles, drained
- 1 cup canned corn, drained

DIRECTIONS

Preheat the oven to 325°F. Heat water in a large saucepan and boil the chicken cubes until no pink remains. Roll out one dough ball until it is ¼ inch thick and lay it in a 9-inch pie pan. Press dough into the base of the pie pan and set aside. Mix the cooked chicken and salsa in a large bowl until the chicken is coated. Add in the green chiles, corn, and cheese. Stir until combined. Add the mixture to the pie shell and spread to fill. Roll out the second ball of pie dough until it is ¼ inch thick, and carefully place it on top of the chicken mixture, then crimp the edges with your two forefingers to seal the pie. Bake for 35 to 45 minutes or until the top of the pie is golden brown. Remove from the oven and cool before serving.

This is a quick recipe for busy nights, and to make it even easier, you could use a store-bought rotisserie chicken. One of my favorite things is looking at a reci-PIE and seeing how I could tweak it or use what I have.

WHAT IN THE HEE HAW PIE

PREP TIME: 45 minutes **BAKE TIME:** 45 minutes

YIELD: 1 (9-inch) pie

INGREDIENTS

1 (1 lb.) Royers herb dough ball (page 12) or 9-inch unbaked pie shell
1 T. butter
1 T. chopped garlic
1 medium red onion, sliced
1 cup ground sausage
½ pound bacon, cut into pieces
1 T. canned chopped jalapeños
1 cup shredded cheddar
4 eggs
¾ cup heavy whipping cream

DIRECTIONS

Preheat the oven to 325°F. Roll out the dough ball until it is ¼ inch thick and lay it in a 9-inch pie pan. Press dough into the base of the pie pan and crimp the edge with your two forefingers. In a sauté pan over medium heat, melt the butter. Add in the garlic and onion, and sauté until transparent. Transfer to a medium bowl and set aside. In the same pan, sauté the sausage and bacon until cooked through. Add the bacon, sausage, jalapeños, cheddar, eggs, and whipping cream to the bowl of onion and garlic. Mix and pour into your pie shell. Bake for 45 minutes.

One of my dearest friends, Susan, a.k.a. Sooze, would always say, "What in the hee haw?" to anything unique or crazy! When I made this for the first time, that is precisely what I said, "What in the hee haw?" I'm sure you will too. It's a beautiful pie for breakfast, lunch, or dinner.

VEGGIE PIE

PREP TIME: 20 minutes **BAKE TIME:** 45 minutes

YIELD: 1 (9-inch) pie

INGREDIENTS

1 (1 lb.) Royers herb dough ball (page 12) or 9-inch unbaked pie shell
¼ cup diced red onion
½ cup chopped mushrooms
1 T. dill butter (page 89)
5 oz. frozen spinach, thawed and drained
2 eggs
2 oz. feta cheese crumbles
2 slices American cheese, torn into pieces
2 slices Swiss cheese, torn into pieces
1 cup shredded cheddar
½ cup sun-dried tomatoes, drained and chopped
½ cup milk
½ cup flour
½ T. Worcestershire sauce
½ T. Mrs. Dash

DIRECTIONS

Preheat the oven to 325°F. Roll out the dough ball until it is ¼ inch thick and lay it in a 9-inch pie pan. Press dough into the base of the pie pan and crimp the edge with your two forefingers. In a small skillet on medium heat, sauté the onion and mushrooms in the dill butter until onion is translucent. Set aside. In a separate bowl, combine all remaining ingredients and mix well. Stir in sautéed vegetables and pour mixture into the pie shell. Bake for 45 minutes.

This is a fabulous pie, even if you're not a vegetarian! When we added savory pies to the menu at Royers Pie Haven, we wanted our customers to have a vegetarian option . . . eat pie for lunch and pie for dessert. Even though it's just a vegetable pie, the flavors are robust and deep!

Remember, like jeans sizes, one 9-inch pie pan may not equal another. Some are deeper, some are shallower, and some are just right. I always keep a stack of foil pie pans around because they are more consistent, and you can give them away. You don't have to worry about getting that cute ceramic pie plate back.

TWICE-BAKED POTATO PIE

PREP TIME: 30 minutes **BAKE TIME:** 45 minutes

YIELD: 1 (9-inch) pie

INGREDIENTS

1 (1 lb.) Royers herb dough ball (page 12) or 9-inch unbaked pie shell
2 lbs. russet potatoes, peeled and cut into large chunks
¼ lb. bacon, chopped
½ yellow onion, diced
½ tsp. garlic powder
½ tsp. lemon pepper
½ tsp. black pepper
½ cup butter
8 oz. cream cheese
1 cup shredded cheddar, divided
¼ cup chopped green onions

DIRECTIONS

Preheat the oven to 325°F. Fill a large pot with water, add potatoes, and boil. In a separate sauté pan, fry the bacon. Remove once cooked, allow it to cool, and then crumble or chop the bacon into bits. Roll out the dough ball until it is ¼ inch thick and lay it in a 9-inch pie pan. Press dough into the base of the pie pan and crimp the edge with your two forefingers. After the potatoes are soft, drain water and mash. Add the onion, garlic powder, lemon pepper, black pepper, butter, cream cheese, and ½ cup of the cheddar. Pour into your pie crust and top with the cooked bacon bits, green onions, and remaining cheese. Bake for 45 minutes or until the cheese is bubbly.

Oh boy, this is such a wonderful meal or side dish. Grill some steaks and serve a slice of Twice-Baked Potato Pie as your side. Do I really need to say more?

BREAKFAST IDEAS

{A Dash of Joy in the Morning}

I remember growing up and setting my alarm to get up at 10 a.m.; oh my gee, I don't think I could sleep until 10 a.m. now if I took two melatonin at 6 a.m. As we grow in our walk with Christ, our desire to sit at His feet takes root, and the roots grow deeper and deeper. But, for the roots to grow deeper, we must let Him prune and water us. We have to make room for the King to do His work in and through us. My alarm goes off around 4:45 a.m. Sometimes, I don't need an alarm. My feet hit the floor, and the enemy says, "Dang it, she's up to put on the full armor of Christ!" Waking up before everyone in the house is my joy in the morning. I light my Junkberry candle from Royers Pie Haven, turn on my favorite worship music, and let Him lead. Every morning is different; sometimes, I paint. Other times, I write down what's on my heart and mind. But my favorite thing is to open His Word and water my roots. These recipes are sweet dashes of joy to savor while you sit at His feet or maybe, share around the breakfast table with your family. Is there someone you have wanted to share with what God is doing in your life? Invite them for coffee and let the Lord move through a blueberry lemon muffin. He can and will reveal Himself through gathering around the table.

BOBBI'S BISCUITS

PREP TIME: 25 minutes **BAKE TIME:** 25 minutes

YIELD: 16 biscuits

INGREDIENTS

3 lbs. breakfast sausage
6 cups Bisquick
1½ cups buttermilk
6 eggs
1 cup pickled jalapeños, sliced
6 cups shredded cheese

DIRECTIONS

Preheat the oven to 300°F. In a sauté pan over medium heat, cook the sausage until no pink remains; drain off grease. In a large mixing bowl, combine the Bisquick, buttermilk, and eggs. Add the sausage, jalapeños, and cheese and combine. Spray a 16-cup muffin pan with cooking spray and fill each cup two-thirds full with the sausage and egg mixture. Bake for 5 minutes, then turn the oven to 275°F and bake for an additional 20 minutes.

A regular biscuit needs butter, jelly, and maybe some honey butter. A Bobbi's biscuit needs nothing added to it! When your biscuit comes with sausage, cheese, and jalapeños, what else does it need? Pull one out of the freezer, pop it out of the foil pan, zap for 30 seconds on each side, and . . . ta-da! Biscuit perfection has been obtained in the unique Tex-Mex way! Who's Bobbi? We met many years ago at table 9 at the café. Bobbi was moving her family to Round Top from Pasadena. Bobbi joined our team, and at one point or another, nearly all her kiddos and their spouses have worked with us!

Did you know you can use milk and white vinegar if you don't have buttermilk? I never have buttermilk at home; if I do, it's incredibly expired. Use 1 cup of milk to 1 teaspoon of vinegar, or ½ cup of milk to ½ teaspoon of vinegar—you get the idea!

BRAND
STEELCUT

BREAKFAST TACO CASSEROLE

PREP TIME: 30 minutes **BAKE TIME:** 15 minutes

YIELD: 6 servings

INGREDIENTS

2 lbs. breakfast sausage
12 eggs
1 lb. Kraft Velveeta, cubed
1 (10 oz.) can RO*TEL, any variety
1 (15.25 oz.) can corn, drained
1 (15 oz.) can black beans, rinsed and drained
½ cup diced red onion
½ cup chopped fresh cilantro
12 tortillas

DIRECTIONS

Preheat the oven to 325°F. In a large skillet, cook sausage and crumble. Crack the eggs into a medium bowl and whisk. When the sausage is no longer pink, pour in the eggs and cook until the eggs are scrambled. Set aside. In a large saucepan over low heat, add Velveeta, RO*TEL, corn, and beans; cover. As cheese begins to melt, stir until all is melted and combined. Add in the onion and cilantro. Set aside. Coat a 9 × 13-inch pan with cooking spray. Fill each of your tortillas with the sausage and egg mixture and place in the baking dish. Cover with cheese mixture, cover pan with foil, and bake for 15 minutes. Enjoy!

This is my go-to breakfast casserole for when the boys have friends over. It's simple, quick, and fills you up! It would also be great for dinner.

CINNAMON ROLL FRENCH TOAST CASSEROLE

PREP TIME: 24 hours **BAKE TIME:** 40 minutes

YIELD: 9 to 12 servings

INGREDIENTS

Casserole

12 slices white bread, torn into pieces
6 eggs
1½ cups half-and-half
¾ cup milk
2 T. sugar
1 tsp. vanilla
½ tsp. ground cinnamon
½ tsp. ground nutmeg
Dash of salt

Praline Topping

2 T. butter, melted
¾ cup brown sugar
¾ cup chopped pecans
4 tsp. corn syrup
½ tsp. cinnamon
½ tsp. nutmeg

I love preparing this casserole on Friday night and having it ready for the weekend. It's great for a Sunday brunch with Bobbi's Biscuits, fresh fruit, and Tara's Cinnamon Whipped Cream.

DIRECTIONS

Coat your 9 × 13-inch pan with cooking spray and place bread in the baking dish. Set aside. In a large mixing bowl, combine the eggs, half-and-half, milk, sugar, vanilla, cinnamon, nutmeg, and salt. Whisk mixture until blended but not too bubbly. Pour mixture evenly over the bread slices in the pan, ensuring all are covered. Cover with foil and refrigerate overnight.

The following day, preheat the oven to 325°F. Prepare the praline topping by mixing the butter, brown sugar, pecans, corn syrup, cinnamon, and nutmeg together. Spread the praline topping evenly over the bread and egg mixture and bake for 40 minutes until fluffy and lightly golden. Serve with maple syrup.

Pie gets them in the door: Pie brings them to us so that we can love them and show them Jesus.

HAVENLY GRANOLA

PREP TIME: 20 minutes **BAKE TIME:** 60 minutes

YIELD: 12 servings

INGREDIENTS

¾ cup dried cranberries
3 cups old-fashioned oats
½ cup unsweetened coconut flakes
¼ cup pecans
1 tsp. ground cinnamon
½ cup honey
⅓ cup crunchy peanut butter

Oh boy, this granola is truly from heaven. When we were in the early planning stages of opening Royers Pie Haven, we wanted to be open for delectable breakfast treats without making bacon and eggs. A dear friend, Mandy Barnard, shared her granola recipe with us, and it's still a staple around here!

DIRECTIONS

Preheat the oven to 275°F. Place the dried cranberries in a small glass measuring cup, cover with water, and microwave for 2 minutes; set aside until plump. Drain cranberries and reserve ¼ cup of liquid. Combine the oats, coconut, pecans, cinnamon, and cranberries in a medium bowl. In a small sauté pan on low heat, stir the honey, peanut butter, and reserved cranberry water until warm and smooth. Pour the liquid mixture over the dry ingredients and mix thoroughly. Spread onto a lined baking sheet. Bake for 60 minutes.

APPLE PIE MUFFINS

PREP TIME: 20 minutes **BAKE TIME:** 40 minutes

YIELD: 12 muffins

INGREDIENTS

3 cups flour
1⅛ cups sugar
5 tsp. baking powder
¾ tsp. salt
1 egg
1 cup milk
¼ cup vegetable oil
4 cups peeled and diced Granny Smith apples
1 cup Streusel Topping (page 16)

DIRECTIONS

Preheat the oven to 375°F. Combine the flour, sugar, baking powder, and salt in a large mixing bowl. Whisk in the egg, milk, and vegetable oil. Fold in the apples. Scoop evenly into 12 greased muffin liners, sprinkle with Streusel Topping, and let rise for 15 minutes. Bake for 10 minutes (this gives a dome top and will not spread). Turn trays around, turn the temp down to 275°F, and bake for an additional 30 minutes (this allows the inside to continue to bake without turning too brown).

Did you know there are over 2,500 apple varieties in the United States? No? Me neither. Even though I love to use Granny Smith apples in this recipe, they could easily be replaced with whatever apples might be on your counter. Granny Smiths are excellent for baking because they never waver in their tartness, flavor, and firmness, just like Granny. This recipe is perfect for a quick-and-easy breakfast in the morning and is guaranteed to wake everyone up with a sweet aroma.

BLUEBERRY LEMON MUFFINS

PREP TIME: 20 minutes **BAKE TIME:** 40 minutes

YIELD: 24 muffins

INGREDIENTS

Batter

6 cups flour
3 cups sugar
2 tsp. salt
2 T. plus 2 tsp. baking powder
4 cups blueberries, fresh or frozen
1⅓ cups buttermilk
1⅓ cups vegetable oil
4 eggs
4 tsp. vanilla

Lemon Cream Cheese Filling

8 oz. cream cheese, softened
½ cup powdered sugar
1 tsp. vanilla
1 T. lemon juice
1 egg
½ cup flour
1 tsp. lemon zest

DIRECTIONS

Preheat the oven to 375°F. In a large mixing bowl, mix the flour, sugar, salt, and baking powder, and fold in the blueberries until coated. In a separate bowl, combine the buttermilk, oil, eggs, and vanilla. Gently fold wet ingredients into the dry ingredients (do not overmix or it will be bready instead of light). Let it sit for 15 minutes to ensure muffins will rise in the middle and not have flat tops.

While the batter is resting, fill 24 muffin cups with liners and spray with baking spray. Make filling: Add all ingredients to a stand mixer (or a large bowl and good ole hand mixer) and blend until thoroughly mixed. Once the batter is done resting, don't stir it. Scoop and fill the bottom of each muffin cup one-third full with batter, then add a spoonful of lemon filling and top with more batter. The muffin cups will be about two-thirds full.

Bake for 10 minutes (this gives a dome top and will not spread). Turn trays around, turn the temperature down to 275°F, and bake for an additional 30 minutes (this allows the inside to continue to bake without turning too brown).

I love to take a menu item that has done well, one that customers would be disappointed if it were taken off the menu, and make it better. This muffin has so much flavor and is a customer favorite, but I wanted to make it O.M.P. I added our lemon cream cheese from the Blueberry Lemon Pie to the muffin batter, and now it's O.M.P.

CHOCOLATE-COVERED-STRAWBERRY MUFFINS

PREP TIME: 25 minutes **BAKE TIME:** 35 minutes

YIELD: 18 muffins

INGREDIENTS

6 cups flour
3 cups sugar
2 tsp. salt
2 T. plus 2 tsp. baking powder
4 cups chopped fresh strawberries
2 cups chocolate chips
1⅓ cups buttermilk
1⅓ cups vegetable oil
5 eggs
4 tsp. vanilla

DIRECTIONS

Preheat the oven to 375°F. Combine the flour, sugar, salt, baking powder, strawberries, and chocolate chips in a large mixing bowl. Set aside. Whisk together the buttermilk, vegetable oil, eggs, and vanilla in a separate bowl. Gently fold liquids into dry ingredients, stirring just enough to moisten all the dry ingredients (do not overmix or it will be bready instead of light). Let mixture sit in the freezer for 15 minutes to ensure muffins will rise in the middle and not have flat tops. Grease 18 muffin cups. Gently scoop mixture into prepared muffin tins; do not stir, as this will break the bubbles starting to form in the rising process. Bake for 10 minutes; this gives the muffins a dome top that won't spread. Turn trays around, turn down the temperature to 275°F, and bake for an additional 25 minutes; this allows the inside to continue to bake without turning the outside too brown. Check for doneness with a toothpick.

Who doesn't love breakfast in bed? These would be perfect for Valentine's morning or an anniversary! I promise you will get extra points for these muffins. P.S. These are great individually wrapped in plastic wrap, stored in a ziplock bag, and frozen.

GRANNY'S CRANBERRY MUFFINS

PREP TIME: 20 minutes **BAKE TIME:** 35 minutes

YIELD: 12 muffins

INGREDIENTS

Batter

2 cups flour
½ tsp. baking soda
1 cup sugar
½ tsp. salt
1 egg
2 T. butter, melted
¾ cup orange juice
1 cup fresh cranberries
½ cup pecan pieces

Drizzle

1 cup powdered sugar, sifted
¼ cup butter, melted
¼ cup orange juice

DIRECTIONS

Preheat the oven to 375°F. Combine the flour, baking soda, sugar, and salt in a large mixing bowl. Fold in the egg, butter, and orange juice. Fold in cranberries and pecan pieces. Grease or line 12 muffin cups. Scoop batter into prepared muffin pans and let rise for 15 minutes. Bake for 10 minutes; this gives the muffins a dome top that won't spread. Turn trays around, turn down the temperature to 275°F, and bake for an additional 25 minutes; this allows the inside to continue to bake without turning the outside too brown. While the muffins are baking, prepare the drizzle: In a small bowl, combine the powdered sugar, butter, and orange juice and whisk until smooth. Drizzle on muffins when cooled.

Many of my favorite childhood memories are baking alongside my granny. I remember traveling to the Texas Hill Country, and I knew we were close when we topped the hill and saw the Burnet Water Tower. We loved to put our aprons on and make a mess in the kitchen, laughing and being silly. This recipe is one I cherish. If I could find her tea cake recipe, you would have it too!

CHOCOLATE CREAM CHEESE BANANA MUFFINS

PREP TIME: 25 minutes **BAKE TIME:** 30 minutes

YIELD: 24 muffins

INGREDIENTS

3 T. espresso powder
4 cups flour
1½ cups sugar
2 tsp. baking soda
1 tsp. salt
2 tsp. cinnamon
1 tsp. nutmeg
3 bananas, mashed
4 eggs
1 cup vegetable oil
1 cup buttermilk
2 T. honey
2 tsp. vanilla

Cream Cheese Filling

24 oz. cream cheese, softened
2¼ cups powdered sugar
1 T. vanilla
2 cups chocolate chips

DIRECTIONS

Preheat the oven to 300°F. Combine the espresso powder, flour, sugar, baking soda, salt, cinnamon, and nutmeg in a large mixing bowl. Add the mashed bananas, eggs, oil, buttermilk, honey, and vanilla and mix well. In a stand mixer, beat the cream cheese, powdered sugar, vanilla, and chocolate chips. Let it sit for 15 minutes to ensure muffins will rise in the middle and not have flat tops. Grease 24 muffin cups. Fill each prepared muffin cup halfway full with the banana mixture, then add a tablespoon of the cream cheese filling into the middle, then divide remaining banana mixture evenly among the cups. Bake for 30 minutes.

This muffin started one day when one of our friends' daughters, Aubrey, asked if she could help make breakfast with me. We never really knew who would show up for coffee or breakfast at our house, which is my favorite; however, on this particular morning, I wasn't expecting company, so we went to the kitchen and started just pulling out ingredients. These banana muffins are what we came up with, and now they are a staple around here.

JUNKBERRY PIE MUFFINS

PREP TIME: 45 minutes **BAKE TIME:** 35 minutes
YIELD: 12 muffins

INGREDIENTS

2¾ cups flour
½ tsp. baking soda
2½ tsp. baking powder
¼ tsp. salt
1 egg
½ cup vegetable oil
1 recipe Junkberry Pie Filling (page 55)
1 recipe Junkberry Pie Topping (page 55)
Sugar for topping

DIRECTIONS

Preheat the oven to 375°F. Combine the flour, baking soda, baking powder, and salt in a large mixing bowl. Fold in the egg, vegetable oil, and Junkberry Pie Filling. Grease 12 muffin cups. Scoop batter evenly into prepared muffin pans, top each with a scoop of Junkberry Pie Topping, and sprinkle with sugar. Let rise for 15 minutes. Bake for 10 minutes; this gives the muffins a dome top that won't spread. Turn trays around, turn down the temperature to 275°F, and bake for an additional 25 minutes; this allows the inside to continue to bake without turning the outside too brown.

You can have pie for breakfast, but when muffins and pie collide, it's a PIE-fect marriage! Our Junkberry Pie Filling swirls in our delish muffin base and is then topped with the sour cream topping and a bit of extra sugar.

PECAN PIE MUFFINS

PREP TIME: 15 minutes **BAKE TIME:** 40 minutes
YIELD: 18 muffins

INGREDIENTS

3 cups flour
4 cups brown sugar
2 T. baking powder
2⅔ cups butter, melted and slightly cooled
2½ T. vanilla
8 eggs
4 cups pecan pieces

DIRECTIONS

Preheat the oven to 375°F. Combine the flour, brown sugar, baking powder, butter, vanilla, eggs, and pecans in a large mixing bowl. Grease 18 muffin cups. Scoop batter evenly into prepared muffin pans. Bake for 10 minutes; this gives the muffins a dome top that won't spread. Turn trays around, turn down the temperature to 275°F, and bake for an additional 30 minutes; this allows the inside to continue to bake without turning the outside too brown.

Did you know Texas is one of the top states for pecan production? That's PUH-KAAN, not PEE-CAN! I love this muffin with a hot cup of coffee, sitting on the back porch with my Bible and journal.

PUMPKIN CREAM CHEESE MUFFINS

PREP TIME: 25 minutes **BAKE TIME:** 40 minutes
YIELD: 24 muffins

INGREDIENTS

Muffin Batter
6 cups flour
3½ cups sugar
1 T. pumpkin pie spice
2 tsp. cinnamon
2 tsp. salt
2 T. plus 2 tsp. baking powder
5 eggs
1⅓ cups milk
1⅓ cups vegetable oil
4 cups pumpkin puree

Cream Cheese Filling
16 oz. cream cheese, softened
1½ cups powdered sugar
2 tsp. vanilla

Streusel Topping
¾ cup brown sugar
¾ cup flour
1 T. cinnamon
½ cup butter, chilled and cut into pieces

DIRECTIONS

Preheat the oven to 375°F. Combine the flour, sugar, pumpkin pie spice, cinnamon, salt, and baking powder. In a separate medium bowl, mix the eggs, milk, oil, and pumpkin puree well and set aside. Gently fold wet ingredients into the dry ingredients (do not overmix, or muffins will be bready instead of light). Let sit for 15 minutes to ensure muffins will rise in the middle and not have flat tops.

While the batter is resting, make the filling: In a stand mixer, cream the cream cheese, powdered sugar, and vanilla. In another bowl, make the streusel topping: Combine the brown sugar, flour, and cinnamon. Cut in butter until mixture is crumbly.

Fill 24 muffin cups with liners and spray with cooking spray. Scoop and fill the bottom of each cup one-third full with pumpkin batter, then add a spoonful of cream cheese filling and top with more batter. The muffin cups will be about two-thirds full. Sprinkle the streusel topping evenly over the muffins.

Bake for 10 minutes; this gives the muffins a dome top that won't spread. Turn trays around, turn down the temperature to 275°F, and bake for an additional 30 minutes; this allows the inside to continue to bake without turning the outside too brown.

This recipe is a cherished fall treat! Not only is it a must with customers, but the pie chicks can't wait for this muffin to come back. The cream cheese filling and streusel topping take this muffin to O.M.P., a.k.a. Oh My Pie! Remember, you can freeze these too, and pull them out as needed. Let thaw overnight or eat frozen—you're welcome!

BERRY SCONES

PREP TIME: 20 minutes **BAKE TIME:** 20 minutes

YIELD: 6 scones

INGREDIENTS

4 cups flour
3 T. sugar plus extra for sprinkling
4 tsp. baking powder
½ tsp. salt
½ tsp. cream of tartar
¾ cup cold butter
1 egg
1½ cups half-and-half
¾ cup raspberries, frozen or fresh
¾ cup blueberries, frozen or fresh

DIRECTIONS

Preheat the oven to 425°F. In a large bowl, mix the dry ingredients. Shave in cold butter and work it in with your hands until mixture is crumbly. Add the egg and half-and-half and mix in by hand. Gently fold in the berries. Turn the dough onto a lightly floured surface, form it into a circle about ¾-inch thick, and cut it into six triangles. Sprinkle dough with sugar. Turn the oven down to 300°F, and bake for 20 minutes.

Scones usually don't make the top of the list when you think of pastries. However, this scone is typically the first breakfast item we sell out of on the weekends at the Pie Haven. Pair it with your favorite hot tea and some of Tara's Cinnamon Whipped Cream; it will become a weekly tradition. Wouldn't having a girls' tea birthday party with these scones be fun?

Look ahead so you can plan. I once bought ingredients and expected to throw the recipe together for dinner that night, but I found out it had a 3-hour step that I missed.

PIE IS LOVE
PIE IS LOVE
PIE IS LOVE
PIE IS LOVE

MORE DESSERTS

{A Sweet Dose of Hope}

Growing up, my parents worked hard to ensure our family's needs. We ate cereal for dinner many nights, and we loved going to garage sales in the fancy neighborhoods to get Guess jeans for a quarter. When our family was given the opportunity to take over the Round Top Cafe, we all saw it as a sweet dose of hope—hope in something better. When we moved from Houston to Round Top, a church member left us gas money to get there. A Round Top local gave us a house right across the street from the café until we got our grounding. My parents knew they had to make this work and fought hard for us.

Quickly, the Lord poured out an abundance because of their obedience. The café flourished overnight, and money, fame, and pride began to take root in me. Over the years I put my hope in material things. The café opened many doors, some I should never have walked through. I saw God's grace as I fumbled down the wrong roads. In 2007, it was a busy night at the café, and I recall falling on my knees in despair and weeping from exhaustion. The Lord met me on that greasy kitchen mat. Looking back, I'm grateful that my parents planted a seed that Jesus was my only hope, not selling one more pie or buying another pair of cute shoes. Since that day, the Lord started to work on my life because I gave Him control. He gently released me from many things I chose, and I've seen His steadfast faithfulness. My heavenly Father will let us go down the wrong path until we learn to depend on Him. That submission set me on a journey of peeling back the layers the world has piled on. Jesus is my only hope.

ESPRESSO CREAM CHEESE BROWNIES

PREP TIME: 24 hours + 45 minutes **BAKE TIME:** 35 to 45 minutes

YIELD: 12 brownies

INGREDIENTS

Brownie Batter

¾ cup cocoa powder
¼ tsp. baking powder
4 T. melted butter, divided
¼ cup Clarissa's Cold Brew (page 15)
2 cups sugar
3 eggs
¼ tsp. salt
1 tsp. vanilla
1⅓ cups flour
2 cups chocolate chips

Cinnamon Cream Cheese Filling

12 oz. cream cheese, softened
1½ cups powdered sugar
¼ tsp. vanilla
¼ tsp. cinnamon
1 T. milk

DIRECTIONS

Note: Remember to prep Clarissa's Cold Brew 24 hours in advance. Preheat the oven to 300°F. In a stand mixer, combine the cocoa, baking powder, 2 tablespoons butter, and cold brew. Add in the sugar, eggs, remaining butter, salt, and vanilla. Add the flour and chocolate chips until combined. In a separate bowl, mix the cream cheese, powdered sugar, vanilla, cinnamon, and milk. Grease a 9 × 13-inch pan. Pour half of the brownie mixture into your prepared pan and cover with cinnamon mixture. Top with remaining brownie batter. Bake for 35 to 45 minutes or until edges pull from pan. Cool for 60 minutes before serving . . . if you can wait that long!

A chocolate and coffee lover's dream brownie. When baking this reci-PIE, the brownie will be ooey and gooey in the middle, but trust the process and know that it's done. It's not a brownie you can cut and serve immediately; it needs a little time to settle. Top with Tara's Cinnamon Whipped Cream and fresh fruit. Delish!

TEXAS TRASH RICE KRISPIES TREATS

PREP TIME: 20 minutes

YIELD: 12 servings

INGREDIENTS

1 cup butter, melted
10 oz. marshmallows
5 cups Rice Krispies
½ cup unsweetened coconut
½ cup crushed graham crackers
½ cup crushed pretzels
½ cup chocolate chips
½ cup Kraft caramel bits

DIRECTIONS

Melt the butter in a large saucepan over medium heat. When the butter is nearly melted, add the marshmallows. Stir until marshmallows are nearly melted, and mix in the Rice Krispies. Add the coconut, graham crackers, pretzels, chocolate chips, and caramel bits. Stir until combined. Press into a greased 9 × 13-inch pan.

When you hit a pie out of the ballpark like the Texas Trash, you start experimenting with the combination of pretzels, caramel, chocolate, coconut, and graham crackers. HMMM, I might need to try peanut butter and white chocolate! When ladies come to Royers Pie Haven, they love to take treats home to the kiddos, and everyone loves a Rice Krispies Treat, especially a trashy one! This is one I love to take to Bible studies or make when the kids have friends over.

BLUEBERRY WHITE CHOCOLATE CHIP COOKIES

PREP TIME: 15 minutes **BAKE TIME:** 18 minutes

YIELD: 30 cookies

INGREDIENTS

2 cups butter, softened
2 cups sugar
2 eggs
1 T. vanilla
1 tsp. salt
1 tsp. baking soda
6 cups flour
2 cups white chocolate chips
1½ cups blueberries, fresh or frozen

DIRECTIONS

Preheat the oven to 275°F. In a stand mixer, cream the butter and sugar until light and fluffy. Mix in the eggs, vanilla, salt, and baking soda. Slowly scoop in the flour and combine. Fold in the white chocolate chips and blueberries, being careful not to squish the blueberries. Line two large cookie sheets with parchment paper. Scoop about 2 ounces of dough (or a generous tablespoonful) and drop about 2 inches apart on the cookie sheets. Bake for 18 minutes.

This is a fantastic cookie to bake for a new neighbor or lazy pool days. I love the white chocolate in this cookie; it's not overly sweet and enhances the flavor of the blueberries. Here's a quick make-ahead tip: Scoop dough into balls on a sheet pan and freeze it. Once the dough balls are frozen, transfer them to a ziplock bag and store in the freezer to bake whenever guests come over.

When baking cookies, as you begin to smell the aroma, the cookies should begin to crack. That means they are almost done!

CHAI COOKIES

PREP TIME: 15 minutes **BAKE TIME:** 18 minutes

YIELD: 36 cookies

INGREDIENTS

2 cups butter, softened
2 cups brown sugar
2 cups sugar
3 eggs
4 tsp. vanilla
1 tsp. baking soda
1 tsp. salt
6 cups flour

4½ tsp. ground ginger
1 T. cinnamon
1½ tsp. allspice
¾ tsp. nutmeg
¾ tsp. cardamom
⅜ tsp. cloves
Scant ¼ tsp. ground black pepper

DIRECTIONS

Preheat the oven to 275°F. In a stand mixer, cream the butter and sugars. Add the eggs and vanilla and mix well. In a separate bowl, combine the dry ingredients and slowly add them to the creamed mixture. Line baking sheets with parchment paper and scoop about 2 ounces of dough (or a generous tablespoonful) and drop dough balls about 2 inches apart on the cookie sheets. Bake for 18 minutes. If you don't want to bake all of them, freeze the remaining balls in the freezer until ready.

When we had the opportunity to open Royers Pie Haven in Henkel Square, we knew we would need dreamy coffee drinks to accompany the pies and treats. Rick and I knew nothing about coffee, but we learned how to work that fancy espresso machine real quick! Now we have a full coffee bar to accompany all our pies and treats! I love the spices of a chai latte, which inspired this cookie.

Tara-rize:
Put my creative spin on it!

CHOCOLATE-COVERED-RASPBERRIES COOKIES

PREP TIME: 20 minutes **BAKE TIME:** 20 to 25 minutes

YIELD: 36 cookies

INGREDIENTS

2 cups butter, softened
2 cups sugar
3 eggs
1 T. vanilla
1 tsp. salt
1 tsp. baking soda
½ cup raspberry puree
6 cups flour
2 cups chocolate chips
1½ cups raspberries, fresh or frozen

DIRECTIONS

Preheat the oven to 275°F. In a stand mixer, cream the butter and sugar until light and fluffy. Add the eggs, vanilla, salt, baking soda, and raspberry puree, then mix. Add the flour and mix. Stir in chocolate chips, then gently fold in raspberries, being careful not to squish the berries. Line two large cookie sheets with parchment paper. Scoop about 2 ounces of dough (or a generous tablespoonful) and drop dough balls about 2 inches apart on cookie sheets. Bake for 20 to 25 minutes until the underside edges of the cookies turn golden brown.

Did you know I was an extra in *Miss Congeniality*? Looking closely at the audience in the pageant scene, you can see my Texas-sized hair. In the scene, pageant hopeful Cheryl Frasier says the perfect date is April 25th. My idea of a perfect date would be eating these cookies with Rick on the back porch in our hammock swing. Here's a quick make-ahead tip: Scoop dough into balls on a sheet pan and freeze it. Once the dough balls are frozen, transfer them to a ziplock bag and store in the freezer to bake for whenever guests arrive.

PEANUT BUTTER AND JELLY COOKIES

PREP TIME: 15 minutes **BAKE TIME:** 18 minutes

YIELD: 12 cookies

INGREDIENTS

1 egg
½ cup butter, softened
½ cup brown sugar
⅓ cup sugar
1 tsp. vanilla
¼ tsp. salt
½ cup peanut butter
1 cup old-fashioned oats
¾ cups flour
¾ tsp. baking soda
1 cup butterscotch chips
Favorite jelly

DIRECTIONS

Preheat the oven to 275°F. In a stand mixer, cream the egg, butter, sugars, vanilla, salt, and peanut butter. In a separate bowl, combine the oats, flour, baking soda, and butterscotch chips and slowly scoop into the creamed mixture. Mix until combined, but don't overbeat. Grease a cookie sheet. Divide the dough into 24 equal-sized balls and place 12 on your prepared cookie sheet. Add a dab of jelly to each cookie and top with the remaining dough balls. Press down to cover the jelly. Bake for 18 minutes. If the dough looks a tad unbaked, that is just right!

Before moving to Round Top, there were days when our family didn't know where the next meal would come from. Peanut butter and jelly sandwiches and cereal were part of the daily routine, so I did not eat either for many years. Many years later, I ate a peanut butter and jelly sandwich and was quickly reminded of how good they are in flavor and sustenance. This cookie is a shout-out to a good ole peanut butter and jelly sandwich! And I'm a grape jelly girl all the way!

MONSTER COOKIE PIE-WICH

PREP TIME: 12 minutes **BAKE TIME:** 18 minutes

YIELD: 12 pie-wiches

INGREDIENTS

Monster Cookies

½ cup butter, softened
1 cup sugar
1¼ cups brown sugar
¾ tsp. vanilla
3 eggs
¾ tsp. corn syrup
2 tsp. baking soda
1½ cups creamy peanut butter
4½ cups oats
½ cup chocolate chips
¾ cup M&M's

Buttercream Frosting

1 cup butter, softened
4½ cups powdered sugar
2 tsp. vanilla
2 T. milk

DIRECTIONS

Preheat the oven to 275°F. In a stand mixer, cream the butter and sugars until light and fluffy. Add the vanilla, eggs, corn syrup, and baking soda and mix well. Add the peanut butter, oats, chocolate chips, and M&M's. Line two large cookie sheets with parchment paper. Scoop about 2 ounces of dough (or a generous tablespoonful) and drop dough balls about 2 inches apart on cookie sheets. Bake for 18 minutes. While baking, combine the buttercream frosting ingredients in a mixer and set aside. Once the cookies are done baking, let them cool completely; turn over 12 cookies and add a generous scoop of buttercream frosting, then add another cookie on top to form a Monster Cookie pie-wich.

If you've never had a monster cookie, you are in for a treat! These cookies are a meal, with peanut butter, oats, and chocolate. What is a pie-wich? It's our version of a cookie sandwich. If you don't want to make them into pie-wiches, skip the buttercream and enjoy the cookies. But don't!

SNICKERDOODLE COOKIES

PREP TIME: 20 minutes **BAKE TIME:** 18 minutes

YIELD: 36 cookies

INGREDIENTS

2 cups butter, softened
2 cups brown sugar
2 cups sugar
3 eggs
4 tsp. vanilla
6 cups flour
1 tsp. baking soda
1 tsp. salt

Snickerdoodle Coating

½ cup sugar
½ cup cinnamon

DIRECTIONS

Preheat the oven to 275°F. In a stand mixer, cream the butter and sugars. Add the eggs and vanilla and mix well. In a separate bowl, combine dry ingredients and slowly add them to the creamed mixture. In a small bowl, mix the sugar and cinnamon for the snickerdoodle coating. Line baking sheets with parchment paper and scoop about 2 ounces of dough (or a generous tablespoonful). Roll cookie dough balls in snickerdoodle coating, and drop about 2 inches apart on cookie sheets. Bake for 18 minutes. If you don't want to bake the cookies immediately, here's a quick tip: Scoop dough into balls on a sheet pan and freeze the pan. Once the dough is frozen, transfer dough balls to a ziplock bag and store in the freezer to bake whenever guests arrive.

My mom and I used to go shopping often. We had our usual stores: Nordstrom for shoes (we loved shoes), Old Navy, and Lane Bryant. We also had lunch at Cheesecake Factory and would stop at Great American Cookies for a Dinky Doozie or a snickerdoodle cookie. I love snickerdoodles: they aren't too rich—just right!

SWEET 'N' SALTY COOKIES

PREP TIME: 15 minutes **BAKE TIME:** 18 minutes

YIELD: 24 cookies

INGREDIENTS

1 cup butter, softened
1½ cups sugar
2 eggs
2 tsp. vanilla
2 cups flour
⅔ cup cocoa powder
¾ tsp. baking soda
½ tsp. salt
1 cup milk chocolate chips
1½ cups Kraft caramel bits
1 T. sea salt

DIRECTIONS

Preheat the oven 275°F. In a stand mixer, cream the butter and sugar. Add the eggs and vanilla and mix until combined. Add the flour, cocoa, baking soda, and salt; mix well. Fold in chocolate chips and caramel bits. Line baking sheets with parchment paper and scoop about 2 ounces of dough (or a generous tablespoonful) and drop dough balls about 2 inches apart on the cookie sheets. Bake for 18 minutes. Sprinkle with sea salt.

I don't remember the year that sweet and salty recipes were trending, but I jumped on the bandwagon, and I am so glad we did. These cookies complement our sweet and salty pie too! If you were to make the cookies and pie next to each other, the flavor profiles would be so different. P.S. Denture wearers, be careful of those thick chunks of caramel!

FRUIT PIZZA

PREP TIME: 20 minutes **BAKE TIME:** 18 minutes
YIELD: 12 to 15 slices

INGREDIENTS

1 (30 oz.) pkg. Pillsbury sugar cookie dough
1 (5.1 oz.) box vanilla instant pudding
2 cups cold milk (for pudding)
2 bananas, sliced
2 cups strawberries, sliced
1 cup green or red grapes, cut in half
2 kiwis, peeled and sliced

DIRECTIONS

Preheat the oven to 275°F. Roll the cookie dough into a 12-inch circle of even thickness and place it on a 12-inch round baking sheet. Bake the cookie dough for about 18 minutes until the edges are light golden brown and center is set. Cool the cookie for about 2 minutes on the pan, then remove to cool completely.

While the cookie is baking, prepare instant pudding according to directions. Once the cookie is cooled, cover with pudding and arrange fruit on top.

Being in the pie business, we don't usually eat pie for dessert. Shocking, I know! My mom would make fruit pizza as dessert often, and my brothers and I loved it! I guess it could be made into pie: press your cookie dough into the pie pan and bake. You will need to place pastry weights in the dough so it doesn't fall. Fill your cookie shell with pudding and top with fruit.

CHOCOLATE-COVERED-CHERRY-PIE SHAKE

PREP TIME: 10 minutes **YIELD:** 1 shake

INGREDIENTS

1 slice cherry pie
2 scoops vanilla ice cream
Chocolate syrup
Splash of milk
Tara's Cinnamon Whipped Cream (page 15)

DIRECTIONS

Combine cherry pie, ice cream, and chocolate syrup in a blender until smooth. Add more milk if it's too thick. Pour into a cold glass and top with Tara's Cinnamon Whipped Cream.

I have always loved to bake, and being in a pie shop helped me stay in my baking lane. I would find delish recipes but knew that they needed to stay pie-related. So, what better way to add a milkshake to the menu than adding pie to it? Any of the pies in this book would be yummy pie shakes, but this is my favorite.

TARA'S CHOCOLATE CHIP COOKIES

PREP TIME: 20 minutes **BAKE TIME:** 18 minutes
YIELD: 36 cookies

INGREDIENTS

- 1 cup butter, softened
- 1 cup shortening
- 1⅓ cups brown sugar
- 1⅓ cups sugar
- 3 eggs
- 2 tsp. white vinegar
- ½ tsp. almond extract
- 4 tsp. vanilla
- 1 tsp. salt
- 2 tsp. baking soda
- 4 cups flour
- 4 cups chocolate chips

DIRECTIONS

Preheat the oven to 275°F. In a stand mixer, cream the butter, shortening, brown sugar, and sugar. Add in the eggs, vinegar, almond extract, and vanilla. Mix in the salt, baking soda, flour, and last, chocolate chips. Line two large cookie sheets with parchment paper. Scoop about 2 ounces of dough (or a generous tablespoonful) and drop about 2 inches apart on cookie sheets. Bake for 18 minutes. If you don't want to bake all the cookies at once, shape remaining dough into balls and line up on a cookie sheet and freeze. Once the dough is frozen, store in a ziplock bag in the freezer and bake as you like!

This cookie can be dangerous because, just like Pringles, once you start you just can't stop. The secret ingredient is the almond extract, trust me on this one. You won't be able to eat just one.

SEASONAL PIES

{A Sprinkle of Celebration}

My mom loved to celebrate and passed that legacy on to me. I love to celebrate ALL THE THINGS. But, as I'm typing this, I realize I truly love celebrating birthdays because that's what Mom would do. Don't get me wrong; I love Thanksgiving dinner, a beautiful wedding with close friends, the birth of a baby, another year of marriage, or graduation. Honestly, milestones are lovely, but what if we celebrated just because? Life gets busy, and we gather to celebrate only the big things. Let's celebrate waking up, a good day at school, a rough day, a child accepting Jesus or repenting quickly. There are so many moments in our daily walk to praise. What if we gathered around the table for a meal and sprinkled in the sweet and savory things we wanted to give thanks for? Selah. Our conversation around the table would be intentional and edifying to Him and us. Let's celebrate because He's been with us through it all. Here are a few ideas to get you going:

- Keep a pen and paper with you and write down all the sprinkles of celebration throughout the day.
- Praise Him.
- Text your friends and family and invite them over for pie and coffee.

Thank You, Lord, for loving us and lavishing Your goodness on us in ALL THINGS!

KAREN'S PUMPKIN PIE

PREP TIME: 15 minutes **BAKE TIME:** 45 to 55 minutes
YIELD: 1 (9-inch) pie

INGREDIENTS

1 (1 lb.) Royers dough ball (page 11) or 9-inch unbaked pie shell
¾ cup sugar
1 (15 oz.) can pumpkin puree
½ cup milk
6 oz. evaporated milk
2 eggs, beaten
2 T. cinnamon
½ tsp. ground ginger
¼ tsp. ground cloves
½ tsp. salt

DIRECTIONS

Preheat the oven to 325°F. Roll out the dough ball until it is ¼ inch thick and lay it in a 9-inch pie pan. Press dough into the base of the pie pan and crimp the edge with your two forefingers. Whisk together the sugar, pumpkin puree, milk, evaporated milk, eggs, cinnamon, ginger, cloves, and salt in a medium bowl. Pour into pie crust. Bake for 45 to 55 minutes until the pie is set in the middle. Let cool before serving.

I am not a girl that gravitates to a pumpkin pie, except my mama's. It has just the right spice and doesn't taste like it came out of a baby food jar, haha! I love it warmed and served with a scoop of vanilla ice cream. Why don't we have pumpkin pie around all year? Let's start a new trend: pumpkin pie 24/7!

O.M.P.: Oh My PIE!

GRANNY'S LEFTOVER TURKEY AND DRESSING PIE

PREP TIME: 20 minutes (much longer if you don't start with leftovers)

BAKE TIME: 45 minutes **YIELD:** 1 (9-inch) pie

INGREDIENTS

1 (1 lb.) Royers herb dough ball (page 12) or 9-inch unbaked pie shell

Cranberry Sauce

½ cup fresh cranberries
1 T. sugar
2 T. orange juice

Stuffing

½ cup butter
1 cup chopped yellow onion
1 cup chopped celery
2 eggs
6 cups white bread, toasted and crumbled
1 (6 oz.) pkg. cornbread, prepared and crumbled
3 T. poultry seasoning
1 tsp. salt
1 tsp. black pepper
4 cups chicken stock
2 cups turkey breast or rotisserie chicken

DIRECTIONS

Preheat your oven to 325°F. Roll out the dough ball until it is ¼ inch thick and lay it in a 9-inch pie pan. Press dough into the base of the pie pan and crimp the edge with your two forefingers. In a small saucepan over medium heat, add the cranberries and cook until they start to open and pop. Then, stir in the sugar and orange juice and continue cooking until the cranberries are soft and the mixture thickens slightly. In a skillet over medium heat, melt the butter and sauté the onion and celery until they turn translucent. Remove from heat and transfer to a large bowl. Stir in the eggs, then add the white bread, cornbread, poultry seasoning, salt, and pepper. Mix everything thoroughly and gradually add in the chicken stock, stirring until the mixture is moist but not soggy. Time to build our pie: pour cranberry sauce on the bottom of the crust, then add turkey or chicken, and top with stuffing. Bake pie for 45 minutes.

Why don't we eat turkey and dressing more than once a year? I always make extra stuffing to make a leftover Thanksgiving pie. My granny's stuffing is the best! Yes, I'm partial, but it is. You could make this with leftover turkey, ham, or chicken.

It's always best to bake your pie on a baking sheet; you don't want all those yummy juices spilling in your oven.

S'MORES ESPRESSO PIE

PREP TIME: 20 minutes **BAKE TIME:** 45 minutes

YIELD: 1 (9-inch) pie

INGREDIENTS

1 (1 lb.) Royers dough ball (page 11) or 9-inch unbaked pie shell

Filling

½ cup butter, melted
½ cup sugar
1 egg
1 tsp. vanilla
½ cup flour
1 tsp. baking powder
¼ cup crushed graham crackers
½ cup chocolate chips
¼ cup chocolate-covered coffee beans, chopped
1 cup miniature marshmallows, divided

Topping

¼ cup brown sugar
½ tsp. vanilla
¼ cup chocolate chips
¼ cup crushed graham crackers
2 T. butter, melted

DIRECTIONS

Preheat the oven to 325°F. Roll out the dough ball until it is ¼ inch thick and lay it in a 9-inch pie pan. Press dough into the base of the pie pan and crimp the edge with your two forefingers. In a stand mixer, cream the butter, sugar, egg, and vanilla. Add in the flour and baking powder. Fold in the graham crackers, chocolate chips, coffee beans, and ½ cup marshmallows, and set aside.

Make topping: Mix the brown sugar, vanilla, chocolate chips, graham crackers, and butter in a separate bowl.

Sprinkle the bottom of the pie crust with the remaining ½ cup of marshmallows, top with pie filling, and finish off with topping. Bake for 45 minutes.

One of my family's fondest memories is visiting Lost Pines Resort in Bastrop, Texas. We go as often as we can. Every evening, the staff fires up two firepits, and families gather around for s'mores. We might eat desserts and figure out how to make it into a pie! What better memory to create a pie in remembrance of sweet family time? I hope your family enjoys this pie around the fire pit!

SWEET POTATO PIE

PREP TIME: 15 minutes **BAKE TIME:** 45 minutes

YIELD: 1 (9-inch) pie

INGREDIENTS

1 (1 lb.) Royers dough ball (page 11) or 9-inch unbaked pie shell
1 (29 oz.) can sweet potatoes
9 T. melted butter, divided
½ cup sugar
1 egg
½ tsp. vanilla
½ cup unsweetened shredded coconut
½ cup brown sugar
½ cup pecan pieces
1 T. flour

DIRECTIONS

Preheat the oven to 325°F. Roll out the dough ball until it is ¼ inch thick and lay it in a 9-inch pie pan. Press dough into the base of the pie pan and crimp the edge with your two forefingers. In a medium mixing bowl, mash the sweet potatoes and add 6 tablespoons of the butter, then sugar, egg, and vanilla. Mix well and pour into the pie shell. Combine the coconut, brown sugar, pecan pieces, remaining butter, and flour in a separate bowl. Add topping to sweet potato mixture and bake for 45 minutes.

Growing up, we hosted Thanksgiving dinner at the café every year. We had packed dinners for pickup on Wednesday and had three seatings on Thanksgiving Day. We would stay in the kitchen all night Tuesday preparing, laughing, making long-lasting memories, and making the most enormous mess. Every Sunday after Thanksgiving, we would close the café and go Christmas shopping together as a family. This reci-PIE is insPIEred by our sweet potato casserole we pass around the table on Thanksgiving.

CHERRY BERRY CINNAMON ROLL PIE

PREP TIME: 20 minutes **BAKE TIME:** 30 to 35 minutes

YIELD: 1 (9-inch) pie

INGREDIENTS

1 (1 lb.) Royers dough ball (page 11) or 9-inch unbaked pie shell

Filling

½ cup butter
1 cup strawberries, fresh or frozen
1 cup pitted cherries, fresh or frozen
1 cup sugar
1 tsp. lemon zest
⅓ cup orange juice
⅓ cup flour
1 cup water
2 cans Pillsbury Cinnamon Rolls

Glaze

1 cup powdered sugar
¼ cup orange juice
¼ cup butter, melted

DIRECTIONS

Preheat the oven to 325°F. Roll out the dough ball until it is ¼ inch thick and lay it in a 9-inch pie pan. Press dough into the base of the pie pan and crimp the edge with your two forefingers. Over medium heat, melt the butter in a large saucepan. Add in the strawberries, cherries, and sugar and cook until the fruit is tender and the mixture thickens. Stir in the lemon zest and orange juice, continuing to stir. In a separate bowl, combine the flour and water and whisk until all flour is dissolved. Add flour mixture to fruit and stir until it thickens. Spoon filling into the crust and top with cinnamon rolls. Bake for 30 to 35 minutes or until the crust is golden. While the pie is baking, make the simple glaze by whisking together the powdered sugar, orange juice, and butter in a small bowl. Once the pie is done, brush on the glaze and dig in!

One year, I got to be in *Where Women Create* magazine and created this signature pie for the editorial and photo shoot. At the time, I probably made cinnamon rolls from scratch, but in my current season of life, cinnamon rolls out of a can are quick and easy. Kids will love this pie, especially with ice cream—YUM!

BRAYDEN'S BANANA BERRY CRISP PIE

PREP TIME: 30 minutes **BAKE TIME:** 45 minutes

YIELD: 1 (9-inch) pie

INGREDIENTS

1 (1 lb.) Royers dough ball (page 11) or 9-inch unbaked pie shell

Pie Filling

4 bananas, sliced
2 cups blueberries, fresh or frozen
1 cup heavy whipping cream
1 cup flour
2 cups brown sugar

Crumble Topping

1 cup brown sugar
¾ tsp. cinnamon
1 cup old-fashioned oats
½ cup flour
⅛ tsp. salt
Pinch of nutmeg
½ cup butter, softened

One Memorial Day weekend, my boys and I were headed to hang out with family at the lake, and I wanted to bring a dessert. We always have bananas about to go bad lying around. I know we can't be the only ones! This is a beautiful pie to take to a summer picnic and serve with ice cream. What isn't good served with ice cream?

DIRECTIONS

Preheat the oven to 325°F. Roll out the dough ball until it is ¼ inch thick and lay it in a 9-inch pie pan. Press dough into the base of the pie pan and crimp the edge with your two forefingers. Fill the pie crust with the bananas and blueberries. In a separate bowl, combine the cream, flour, and brown sugar. Pour over the bananas and blueberries. In another bowl, combine the topping dry ingredients and then stir in butter. Add crumble to the top of the pie, pressing over the filling and covering the whole pie. Bake for 45 minutes or until the topping is golden.

PARADISE MANGO PIE

PREP TIME: 30 minutes **BAKE TIME:** 45 minutes

YIELD: 1 (9-inch) pie

INGREDIENTS

1 (1 lb.) Royers dough ball (page 11) or 9-inch unbaked pie shell

Mango Filling

5 fresh mangos, peeled and cut into chunks

½ cup sugar

1 T. lemon juice

¼ tsp. ground ginger

1 T. cornstarch

Topping

1 cup unsweetened coconut

½ cup brown sugar

½ cup flour

½ cup butter, softened

1 T. vanilla

DIRECTIONS

Preheat the oven to 325°F. Roll out the dough ball until it is ¼ inch thick and lay it in a 9-inch pie pan. Press dough into the base of the pie pan and crimp the edge with your two forefingers. In a braising pot over medium heat, combine the mangos, sugar, lemon juice, and ginger and stir until it bubbles. Mangos don't need to be soft because they will continue cooking in the oven. Add in the cornstarch and stir until mixture thickens; remove from heat. In a separate bowl, make topping: Combine the coconut, brown sugar, and flour. Stir in the butter and vanilla. Pour the fruit filling into your pie pan and spread the topping evenly over the top. Bake for 45 minutes.

When you smell this pie baking in the oven, the aroma takes you to a cozy Adirondack chair on a white sandy beach with a piña colada in your hand. It is as refreshing as an iced cold lemonade on a sweltering Texas summer day.

CHRISTMAS SPIRIT PIE

PREP TIME: 20 minutes **BAKE TIME:** 45 minutes

YIELD: 1 (9-inch) pie

INGREDIENTS

1 (1 lb.) Royers dough ball (page 11) or 9-inch unbaked pie shell

Filling

3 cups cranberries, fresh
3 cups raspberries, fresh
Zest of 1 orange, divided
¾ cup sugar
1 cup orange juice
½ cup flour
1 cup pecan pieces

Topping

1 cup sour cream
1 cup flour
1¼ cups sugar, divided
¼ tsp. salt

DIRECTIONS

Preheat the oven to 325°F. Roll out the dough ball until it is ¼ inch thick and lay it in a 9-inch pie pan. Press dough into the base of the pie pan and crimp the edge with your two forefingers. In a sauté pan over medium heat, combine the fruit and half the zest (reserve the other half for the topping). Stir until it begins to warm. Add the sugar and orange juice and cook until the mixture bubbles. Add the flour and stir until mixture starts to thicken. Stir in the pecans until incorporated.

Make topping: Whisk the sour cream, flour, 1 cup of the sugar, and salt in a separate bowl and set aside. Pour the fruit filling into your pie pan and spread the topping evenly over the top. Sprinkle with the remaining ¼ cup sugar and remainder of the orange zest. Bake for 45 minutes or until the edges are golden brown.

I love walking into the grocery store after the sweltering heat of a Texas summer and seeing pumpkins, gourds, and cranberries—a sign of hope for what's to come. Ever try to describe something by how it smells? This tastes like potpourri in your mouth, but it's not potpourri—THANK GOODNESS!

INDEX

BREAKFAST IDEAS

MORE DESSERTS

SEASONAL PIES

ABOUT THE AUTHOR

Tara Royer Steele has been baking pies for nearly forty years. She is the owner of Royer's Pie Haven in Round Top, Texas. She lives on seven acres in Brenham, Texas, where her commercial kitchen, bake shop, and mail-order business are located as well. She and her husband and business partner, Rick, also hold retreats for men, women, and youth on their property. They are the proud parents of two active boys, Brayden and Bentley.

ABOUT THE PHOTOGRAPHER

Lori Sparkman is an entrepreneur, commercial photographer, and the owner of Lori Sparkman Photography. For more than 15 years she has worked extensively with corporate branding accounts, the fitness industry, weddings, and high-profile clients. Based in Little Rock, Arkansas, Lori is a sought-after traveling photographer and has roamed the world with camera in hand to capture celebrations and special events. Her visual artistry can be seen in local magazines and published books, including *Our Wedding Planner*, *Teatime Discipleship*, and *Well Lived*.

COLD DRINKS
BREAKFAST LUNCH
THE ORIGINAL PIE SHAKE

COFFEE
GLUTEN
COLD DRINKS
BREAKFAST LUNCH
PIES
THE ORIGINAL PIE SHAKE
FRESH ROASTED COFFEE
BAKED GOODS

COLD DRINKS
PIE SHAKE
$10
GLUTEN FREE